THIS BOOK BELONGS TO
The Library of

....

....

COPYRIGHT 2024

The content contained within this book may not be reproduced, duplicated, or transmitted without direct written permission from the author or the publisher. Under no circumstances will any blame or legal responsibility be held against the publisher, or author, for any damages, reparation, or monetary loss due to the information contained within this book. Either directly or indirectly.

Legal Notice:
This book is copyright protected. This book is only for personal use. You cannot amend, distribute, sell, use, quote, or paraphrase any part, or the content within this book, without the consent of the author or publisher.

Disclaimer Notice:
Please note the information contained within this document is for educational and entertainment purposes only. All effort has been executed to present accurate, up-to-date, and reliable, complete information. No warranties of any kind are declared or implied. Readers acknowledge that the author is not engaging in the rendering of legal, financial, medical, or professional advice. The content within this book has been derived from various sources. Please consult a licensed professional before attempting any techniques outlined in this book. By reading this document, the reader agrees that under no circumstances is the author responsible for any losses, direct or indirect, which are incurred as a result of the use of the information contained within this document, including, but not limited to — errors, omissions, or inaccuracies.

Thank you for Purchasing my book and taking the time to read it from front to back. I am always grateful when a reader chooses my work and I hope you enjoyed it!

With the vast selection available online, I am touched that you chose to be purchasing my work and take valuable time out of your life to read it. My hope is that you feel you made the right decision.

I very much would like to know what you thought of the book. Please take the time to write an honest and informative review on Amazon.com. Your experience and opinions will be of great benefit to me and those readers looking to make an informed choice.

With much thanks.

Table of Contents

Introduction	5
Chapter 1: Why You Should Have Multiple Sources of Income	6
Chapter 2: Benefits of Passive Income	15
Chapter 3: How to Make Money from Rental Property	24
Chapter 4: Examples of Passive Income	34
Chapter 5: Online Business Ideas and How to Profit from Them	44
Chapter 6: Why Some People Find It Easier to Create Multiple Streams of Income Than Others	54
Chapter 7: How to Sustain Multiple Streams of Income	63
Chapter 8: Things to Avoid When You Have Multiple Streams of Income	75
Chapter 9: Tips and Tricks of Creating Passive Income	84
Conclusion	94

Introduction

Thank you for downloading "Passive Income: An Essential Guide to Creating Multiple Streams of Income and Building an Empire of Wealth Using Rental Property Investing and Online Business Ideas Such as E-commerce and Blogging."

The rate of inflation is high, and we all need to have a passive income. Having one source of income is counterintuitive because you have nowhere to run to when things become hectic. Have you ever seen those people who are broken when their main sources of income crumble? You don't want to be that person who begs from others because you did not consider having a passive income!

You may be wondering what a passive income is — and how to get started. For starters, a passive income is the money obtained from engaging in resourceful activities other than your main source of income and requires little to no effort. You can earn money while you sleep when you engage in passive income. For example, you can invest in rental properties and put someone in charge or control it yourself. You only need to put measures in place to ensure that it runs effectively. While it may be difficult and confusing at first to start a passive income, it is fulfilling in the end.

However, passive income will not generate income overnight, so hold your horses! Similar to any other source of income, passive income requires patience, hard work, and commitment. Furthermore, you must know where and how to invest. Moreover, passive income can be costly, and that is why you need to know what you are getting yourself into. Taking the time to understand a business before you invest and managing it well can generate good money over time. There are plenty of passive income ideas in 2019, such as investing in real estate, starting a YouTube channel, opening a car wash, and selling used items. Don't be afraid to start a passive income; it may just save you in time of need.

Chapter 1: Why You Should Have Multiple Sources of Income

Having multiple streams of income is no longer an option but a necessity. With the high rate of unemployment, having several sources of income comes in handy, yet despite this, many people rely solely on employment. When they are fired from their workplace, they become depressed and take long to get back' but this should not be the case because there are many ways to make money. Technology has not only simplified life, but also created job opportunities — many people many good monies in the comfort of their homes.

Moreover, little is needed to start earning money online. Therefore, there is no excuse as to why you don't have multiple streams of income. Reasons, why you should have multiple streams of income are discussed below.

You should have multiple streams of income because it diversifies sources of income. Any banker can tell you that diversifying your portfolio helps in reducing risks. If you are willing to diversify your portfolio, why not your income? There are times when sources of income dry up. Diversifying your income helps to lessen risks and cover for a dry spell. It is devastating when you want to pay rent or school fees, and your only source of income is depleted, leaving you with two options: borrow from others or miss making the payment — which only creates more problems. This is why having multiple streams of income comes in handy, as a person with a diversified income rarely has financial issues.

To Curb Unemployment

Everyone is complaining about the high rate of unemployment, but few are doing anything about it. The world has changed, and smart people have realized that they cannot rely solely on their jobs. Waiting for job offers is not wise because you never get to discover your potential, so, instead of finishing school and waiting for job offers, you should consider doing something you love. There are many things you can do and make good money from, and patience is key when starting your search for passive income. It might be hectic at first, but things get better with time. You will soon realize that it is a worthwhile venture, and you can hire people when the business expands. Schools are advised to change people's mentality about sources of income. The era of going to school and applying for jobs is over because jobs are scarce. While employment is not a bad idea, it's wise to not make it your only source of income. If you are not knowledgeable about what business to start, consult career experts. Unemployment should be a thing of the past, given the number of opportunities today. If you do not have the resources, you can collaborate with a friend. However, be careful who choose to work with to avoid making losses. Some people have bad intentions and can dupe you into working with them, taking all the profits. If you decide to start a stream of income with someone, draft a contract, and abide by the terms. Creating streams of income is not as difficult as people make it seem and working with someone makes the decision-making process easy because you have someone to consult.

To Control Your Income

Not everyone gets a raise or promotion in the workplace. It can be tiring if you work hard but receive no appreciation, and some people end up quitting their jobs because of how demanding and frustrating it is. Even if you get a promotion this year, there is no guarantee that you will get it next year. You can avoid that frustration and take control of your career by creating multiple streams of income and having multiple streams of income gives you control of income and resources. You can give yourself a raise anytime you want, and you also the liberty to do things the way you want. There are some employers who pay late or pay in installments, making life difficult for employees because they are forced to borrow money from people to lead meaningful lives. Some employers hold on to salaries to prevent employees from leaving, and employees have no choice but to continue working there in hopes of getting paid. Having multiple streams of income enables you to decide when you get paid and allows you to decide not to take money from a certain investment; instead, you may decide to allow it to grow. You know how the business is doing, when to withdraw money, and when to invest more.

Create a Holiday Fund

We all have places we wish to visit but lack the funds. You might be a new couple that wants to take a break from work and tour the world, but due to tight work schedules and limited resources, you forgo the plans. This can be fixed simply by starting multiple streams of income and then, rather than stressing where you will get the money to visit places you love, you start a holiday fund. Your different streams of income mean that money will be coming in from different sources, and you can direct money from one or two sources to the holiday fund. Moreover, having multiple streams of income eliminates the stress that comes with employment. You can put someone in charge of your business or businesses, monitor the progress of each, and use the extra time to take charge of your life. It also enables you to enjoy your holiday in peace knowing that money is coming in. Moreover, many employees seldom get time to travel because of the nature of their jobs, and their families travel alone most of the time. Such jobs can create a strain on the family and cause a breakdown. Burnout is real, and employees who work continuously without a break are risking their health, and often face endless emotional and social problems. Having multiple streams of income not only enables you to save for holiday, but it also gives you the needed time to rest. It allows you to spend time with loved ones and unwind from hectic work life. You come back with a clear mind, ready to do business, and the days of borrowing money every time you want to travel with your family are over.

To Stick to Your Values

Many businesses today require employees to compromise their values to fit in. Millennials are applauded for sticking to their values more than any other generation. However, when you work in a company which wants you to do certain things you don't believe in, you don't have a lot of options; either you comply or quit. It would be easier to quit if there were a lot of opportunities, but that is not the case. Suddenly you are hit with the fear of staying unemployed for years or settling for less. Many people compromise their values and beliefs to please their employers and some employers do not acknowledge the sacrifice people make to improve the company. All they care about is increasing their profits at the expense of employees' morals. Creating multiple streams of income allows you to engage in activities that don't weigh down on your conscious, giving you peace of mind and the confidence to work hard, and also it leads to satisfaction and self-reliance.

People who realize a great sense of fulfillment are those who work at home. For the longest time, the norm was getting up early, climbing the career ladder, and retiring; now, things have changed drastically, and more people opt to create multiple streams of income, allowing them to work with like-minded people. Any business owner can tell you that working with people who have contrary beliefs and values can cripple the business. Creating multiple streams of income not only allows you to create your own value system but also work with like-minded people. When people have similar values, it becomes easier to achieve goals which have been set.

To Take Risks

Many people do not want to leave employment because they like the comfort it brings. They do not want to take risks of their own. They argue that they are not good at business, but the truth is that they don't want to take risks, and it is only risk-takers who succeed in life.

There is no guarantee that a business decision will bring in profit; all you can do is make decisions and hope for the best. Sometimes such decisions lead to massive gains, but other times they contribute to expected losses. If you are the kind of person who fears taking risks, it will be difficult for you to experience success. Creating multiple streams of income needs a risk-taker. One thing that you can be sure of is that you will make many mistakes in the process, however, you will learn lessons that will make you a better manager.

To Challenge Yourself

The truth is you will not know your full potential unless you try something different. Get out of your comfort zone and start that business you have been thinking of for a while; it may be risky, but that is where you will discover your potential. Instead of staying in a job where you are miserable, challenge yourself by starting a passive income stream. Millennials thrive on adrenaline and things that challenge them, and even companies understand the nature of millennials to switch things around in the offices to appeal to themselves. Millennials have a lot of potential, but it takes dedication to tap into them.

To Pay College Fees

Many students cannot pay their college tuition due to a lack of funds. Make this a distant memory by starting a passive income today. Parents start saving for their children's college fees, but financial issues derail the plans. Instead of using your retirement to save for college fees, why not create an alternative income source to sort that out?

College fees vary across states; take this into consideration, and save yourself the trouble of seeking loans when it is possible for you to get money yourself by finding the right passive income to engage in. Many students drop out of college because their parents did not invest wisely, but students can make money and pay off their tuition fees or debts. If your parents are unable to pay your fees, you can do it yourself. Many young people have started YouTube channels to make money, and if you are creative, there are plenty of way you can take advantage of money-making activities on the internet. Don't give up on your dreams just because your parent is unable to pay your tuition. You can find a part-time job and pursue a college degree. With the high rate of opportunities, there is no excuse to give up. If you decide to venture into an online business, seek advice from people who are successful at it. Also, it will take some time before you gain many followers, so you must be patient and trust in the process. As long as you are doing what you love and trying to improve every day, things will work out in the end. What prevents many people from succeeding is comparing themselves to others. You don't know another person's journey; some have been in the business for a long time that is why they are more successful than you. Others are simply more skilled than you, and that is okay. Keep in mind that you are doing this business for you, not someone else. When you appreciate your own efforts and maintain the focus, it becomes easy to realize success. If you are in college, live according to your means because there is no point in creating multiple sources of income as a student if you are going to misuse the money. Many students make good money but use it on parties, shopping sprees, and other wasteful adventures. They realize their mistakes when exams are approaching, yet they have not taken care of their fees, and can lose an entire semester's progress. Even if your parent saves up money for your college studies, if you don't know how to use it, it is meaningless. The secret to getting money is using what you have wisely. Spend money on the most important things first and use the balance on indulgences. College students love to have fun, and that is normal, however, don't do it at the expense of your studies. Learn ways to make money to supplement what you are given by your parents; learning how to make money while in school makes it easier for you to adjust to the outside world once you finish school. At the end of the day, what matters is that you finish college and develop a good career. Moreover, you will have a source of income once you finish college. Many students struggle to get jobs after college, depending on their parents, but if you start the YouTube channel early, it can grow to become a good source of income.

To Cater to the Rising Cost of Health

Health reform has led to higher health costs, and people are feeling the pinch. It is extremely difficult for people with small salaries and large families. Many people do not seek healthcare services because they do not have money to pay. Having multiple streams of income caters to the high medical costs and alleviates the burden that comes with it. Instead of waiting for your employer to increase your salary or increase your medical coverage, have an alternative source of income. The government has implemented measures to provide medical care to everyone, but there are limitations. The government has been accused in the past of not doing enough to improve healthcare and there is a huge ongoing debate as to whether the government needs to do more to improve access to healthcare. The good thing is that it is engaging the public on ways to provide services. Creating multiple streams of income guarantees you good medical coverage, and you won't be worrying in case of a medical emergency. Many people are forced to borrow money to pay medical bills accrued over time, some are forced to stay in hospitals longer as their families look for the money or discharged too early because they can't afford the care. Employment can end when you need it the most. Some employers are not understanding and will terminate your contract when you are sick. They will not tell you directly that they don't want to work with you, but instead, they will create issues and blame you for it. You can sue the employer, but it might take time to get compensation for unlawful termination; this can be a big blow if you are sick and in need of medical care. Having other sources of income helps to cover medical expenses when your job ends, so avoid the stress that comes with increased medical costs by having a passive income as medical bills can accrue and become difficult to settle if you don't have a stable job.

To Pay off Debt

If you have ever carried debt, then you know the pressure that comes with it. The lender can demand the money when you least expect it. Many relationships have been broken because of one party failing to honor its debts. While some people have the habit of borrowing and never returning, others genuinely lack money. It is tricky when the lender is not your friend. You might have borrowed money from the bank to complete a project and failed to get it back on it. Failure to clear pending debts has dire consequences and can damage your reputation. Few people opt to forgive the debtor or give them more time. Most of the time, the lender informs the authorities or take things from your house to clear the debt. Avoid the shame that comes with not honoring your debt by creating multiple streams of income, as money coming from various sources makes it easy to clear debts faster. It builds your reputation and makes you reliable; you can pay off your debt slowly, as arranged by the lender. Also consider that having multiple streams of income can allow you, one day, to become a lender.

To Live a Fulfilled Life

The number of people who are unhappy with what they are doing is extremely high. They feel trapped because they have no option but to stay in the current situation, doing a job that is draining and sucks the life out of them. If this is you, you may start being depressed, sad, and unsure about the future. Free yourself from this cage by creating multiple streams of income, do what you want to do, and you no longer are bound by the expectations of your employer. If you are unhappy about your present situation, do something about it instead of complaining. Having multiple streams of income enables you to live a happy and fulfilled life, doing things the way you want without pressure. Moreover, it allows you to take charge of your life and dictate how things are accomplished. People with multiple streams of income attest to its benefits and encourage everyone to join them. Contrary to what many people believe, you don't have to have a lot of resources to start a new venture; all you need is determination and a strong will. It might be tricky at first, but it becomes easy with time.

To Improve the Economy

People are urged to venture into a business to increase their income and boost the economy. Governments rely on the business sector to thrive, and if more people join, it will be easier to lift economies. Some governments offer free training and sponsorship to people who want to create streams of income. Take advantage of such offers to become a good business manager to increase your potential for money-making. The cost of living is high, and the only remedy is to create more opportunities. In this way, having multiple streams of income also helps the economy. If the business sector is stable, the government will no longer have to depend only on external donors or taxes to stay afloat. What is important is to take time to understand every sector and the skills that are needed to thrive. Many people have expressed an interest in starting businesses, and through proper training and guidance, more people will develop an interest in creating multiple streams of income. As they see this approach working, they will drop the attitude of depending solely on employment and begin creating steady incomes for themselves.

Chapter 2: Benefits of Passive Income

Time is too precious to waste it on meaningless gains. You only have 24 hours in a day, and this is why you should be careful how you spend your time. Unlike money which can be spent, lost, and regained, time is irreversible. One of the best ways you can spend your time is finding and maintaining passive income flows. Once you venture into this route, you will never regret it, as it is the only way the wealthy become wealthier. It enables you to achieve more from the limited time you have a day, allowing you to gain more because you are doing different things at the same time. When you are employed by someone else, there are times when you are wasting time the entire afternoon; sitting around and waiting 5 PM to go home. Consider the number of hours you waste in the office sitting idle; you can become rich by creating a passive income, making money in other streams. Many people have heard how easy it is to create and sustain a passive income, but don't know how to get started. Others are afraid of venturing into the unknown and the risks involved. Despite its benefits, passive income is not as easy as many believe. It requires commitment and might take more effort than your regular employment. You have to sacrifice a lot to sustain a passive income, especially if you have many streams. You will experience a lot in the process — which may make or break you. Despite its challenges, passive income is the pathway to wealth and fulfillment. Below are the benefits of passive income

Freedom of Your Time

Time cannot be recovered. You cannot decide to push back time because you misused yesterday. No way. This is why it is important to start passive income today when you have the time. You are free to do what you want when you want. Formal employment is demanding and strips you of any freedom you want. You are supposed to be in the office at a specific time and only leave when work is done, forced to sacrifice time with families to please your boss. Other times you take lengthy job trips and resume work immediately when you return, barely getting time for yourself. The good thing with creating a passive income of income is that you are in charge, deciding to put in a lot of effort in one week and be free the next one. Alternatively, you can opt to put someone in charge, letting them manage the day-to-day duties. Everything is up to you when you have a passive income. However, the convenience provided by passive income does not mean that you are free from your obligations. You still need to put in the work for passive income to generate profits. The only difference between having passive income and one source of income is flexibility; provided that your passive income generates expected income, you are free to spend time on other things. You also need to be careful when choosing who to put in charge. Don't give someone a position just because they express interests or are related to you. If you are going to be away for a long time, it is better to put a professional, reliable, and honest person in charge. You should be able to trust them to make the right decisions and honestly handle the money. Some people have lost entire businesses by putting the wrong person in charge of that business. Don't be deluded by a person's demeanor (some people will say anything and act any way to get the job.) If you are unsure about someone, seek a second opinion. The freedom that comes with passive income should not be misused, so only take a break when after putting everything in order, leaving only when you are sure that you have someone capable in charge. Once your passive income is running smoothly, you can take time to tour the world with your family or do things alone. It is up to you now that you don't have to worry about the money. If you are single, you can decide to settle down and start a family. Freedom of time gives you the freedom of choice.

Reduces Anxiety, Stress, and Fears About the Future

The future is uncertain if you only have one source of income. You could be stranded if you lose your job suddenly and having only one source of income causes much suffering from extreme stress and anxiety. Often, people fear leaving their stressful jobs because they don't have options. If they leave, they have to start from square one, and now they are stressed about providing for their families and climbing the career ladder, again, from the bottom rung. They are dependent on the source of income and compromise on their values regularly.

Nothing is more stressful than being unable to pay your bills. It is even worse if you have children in school and others depending on you, causing frustration and hopelessness. You begin to wonder what will happen if you lose your job and how they would react. It weighs you down physically, emotionally, and socially. You lose hope about the future and stop working hard because all you see is a failure. Whenever we live in fear and anxiety, it is difficult to give our best. We perform poorly because we are not at the moment, and it becomes difficult to enjoy what we have because we are constantly worried about the what-ifs. We are caught up in our thoughts, often losing focus, making it impossible to break the chains binding us; negativity does not help. Passive income alleviates all the worries associated with having only one source of income. Even when one fails, you can relax, knowing that you are covered by the other one. You can live in the moment, enjoying what you have, taking care of your family and feeling good about your achievements. When you are not stressed about your income, you are more effective and productive, getting a lot more accomplished when you know you are relaxed and sure that you have a steady flow of income from different sources. Moreover, you thrive emotionally, physically, and mentally when you have passive income. Have you ever met those who people are constantly down, having no hope in life? Some of them are affected by financial issues in the family. Passive income builds your momentum to achieve more and to make more. It eliminates fears about the future. Secure your future today by starting passive income, because while you might have a good job today, no one knows about the future. Everything may seem to be in place, but things change; smart people know that the future is uncertain, and they take steps to secure it today. They do so by determining how to make money doing what they love. You don't have to do complex things to make a fortune. As a matter of fact, you are more likely to gain more from doing things that you love because you are motivated to work hard when doing things that bring you joy. Don't start passive income because others are doing it because you might realize that it is not the right path for you when it is too late. Instead, take time to assess the passive income to know if it is the right path for you.

While having only one source of income can be stressful, it can also be stressful having multiple sources of income if they are not handled properly. Don't strain yourself in attempts to make multiple small fortunes; if the workload is too much, ask for help. Alternatively, you can postpone some options until you have time. Passive income is enjoyable if done properly.

It Allows You to Do Things That You Love

There are few people who are truly fulfilled with the kind of job they have. Many pursue a career solely for the money – not the love of the job. Passive income allows you to do the things that you love. It leads to satisfaction and happiness. We are all passionate about some things. however, often we postpone doing what we are passionate about due to fear of failure, lack of funds, or opportunities. Whatever the reasons, everyone deserves a chance to do what they love, and we should be free to indulge in our fantasies without reproach or fear of failure. Sadly, not everyone gets a chance to do what they love, being stuck in jobs that they hate, and living with regret for not taking different career paths. Passive income allows you to do what you genuinely care about. Moreover, it frees you to be yourself, allowing for flexibility that lets you create time for your family and yourself. You get to discover who you are, and your purpose.

Passive Income Frees You from Societal Expectations

Who said that you have to go to school, graduate and find employment? Many people want to live up to societal expectations that they forgo their dreams. Some family members feel offended when you don't have multiple streams of income. Others may accuse you of engaging in illegal activities. The most important thing is to have inner peace. As long as you are doing the right thing, there is no to fear in being a free spirit who has the right to be themselves. People who truly care will be right there with you, supporting your passive income endeavors. Passive income shifts your focus from working to pay the bills to living out your purpose. Sadly, there are parents who have unrealistic expectations from their children, and some use their children to fulfill goals they did not achieve themselves. They define the career path the child is supposed to take, and there is no negotiation. Such children grow up miserably because they have no voice, the pressure is too much, and they have no one to turn to. It can be hard standing up to your parents. Others follow their parents' guidelines even when it is not what they want. If you are not comfortable doing something, speak up. The other party may not know that you are not comfortable following that path, thinking that you are both on the same page. Societal expectations hinder many from achieving their dreams. In some societies, it is wrong for women to engage in certain businesses, limiting them to specific roles such as cleaning, cooking, and nurturing. Such women have no support, even from families and friends, to further their dreams. They follow societal expectations and never question anything, and the few that stand up for themselves are often considered outcasts. Society should let people live for themselves.

The worst thing that can happen to a person is to let others dictate their lives. As long as you are happy, don't mind what others say. Passive income is one way of doing what you love, whether society accepts it or not. It is one way of standing up for yourself and being heard. If you have been dreaming of venturing into a certain business, don't let societal expectations hinder you from doing that; stand up and be counted. Many people live miserable lives because they cannot speak their minds, but it is time to change that narrative. The minute you stop caring what the society wants is when you will be truly happy, as success comes when you consider your own feelings, ideas, and interests. This does not make you selfish; it only means that you are not influenced by what others think. In addition, it means you are strong enough to handle what the world throws at you. It can be scary standing up for what you believe in, but that is what will make you successful, separating you from everyone else. People will resist the change, but with time they will accept it, but only when you become immovable in starting your passive income stream and being diligent with it, working hard and telling people why you are doing it. The society may resist it because they don't understand what it entails. Others may have wrong ideas about your source of income, so it's up to you to change their minds and show them the good side of your endeavor. Engaging in a passive income that is frowned upon by society around you can be hectic and hard; it requires strong-willed people to make it successful.

You Can Work Anywhere

The good thing with passive income is that it can be done anywhere when using the internet. You can live anywhere and still get paid! Some people love traveling and cannot stand staying in one place for too long, so with passive income, they can hit the road anytime. You just need to put things in place to facilitate your travels. Unlike a regular job in which you have to stay in a particular place, you are a free bird with passive income. You won't think twice about moving to the place you have always wanted to live. Some people wish to move to new places but cannot because of the nature of their jobs and are forced to stay in places they are not happy. Others live far from work, traveling long commutes every morning. Such travel costs can be high, forcing many to relocate. The good news is that you won't have to travel if you make online jobs your passive income. You can do it anywhere, saving you money you would otherwise spend every day on your commute. You make more by the end of the month than those who wake up every day and start their commute to work outside of their homes or communities.

Economic growth and stability

You can amass a large sum of wealth within a short period. This is true for those with regular jobs and passive income, channeling the money from passive income to a savings account, investing the money once it reaches a certain amount. Passive income leads to financial stability. When you have an automatic income and do not worry about paying bills at the end of the month, you can focus on strengthening your financial position. You have the time to do market research and find areas of investment, assessing market conditions, and making wiser decisions. Passive income makes it easy to deal with life challenges. If you have ever been forced to borrow large sums of money to deal with an emergency, then you know the importance of having an additional, outside income stream. Sometimes challenges arise you don't have money, and if you rely on your job alone, you can be stuck. While problems will still arise from time to time, passive income makes them easy to tackle. Whether you agree or not, passive income is paramount. You can profit greatly from passive income if you don't give up. It gives financial freedom like no other. Moreover, it leads to independence. You stop relying on people and start depending on yourself, making investment decisions alone. Previously, your employer used to do everything, but now the ball is in your court, and while it can be scary at first, soon you learn how to do things. Financial stability contributes to significant growth in other aspects of your life, giving you hope for a better future. There is no reason to fail if you do proper research and invest wisely. It's time to shake off your shackles in terms of having only one source of income, so challenge yourself today to take that step of faith, freeing yourself and your family from the fears of tomorrow.

Offers a Creative Outlet

If you are the kind of person who loves creating things, then passive income is for you. Relying on one source of income can hinder you from exploring your interests, and it's even worse if you work for someone. You cannot incorporate your ideas the way you want, and you must seek permission before you do anything. Sometimes your ideas are rejected because someone else does not believe that they are relevant. If you don't muster the guts to speak up, your creativity goes down the drain. This is why it is crucial to have a passive income that allows you to be who you are. Burnout happens when employees are constantly bombarded with work non-stop; and cannot complain about it because employers think that it is disrespectful for employees to explore their creative side without consulting them. In a way, employers might be right because having their nose in every corner enables them to know everything that is happening in the company. When you have passive income, you can explore different things, eliminating a great deal of possibility for burnout. Your success depends on what you want to do and how to bring your ideas to life; your ideas are not overlooked by a boss, and you are not relying on someone else. Others are not passionate about your beliefs, and that is understandable, so passive income streams allow you to be who you are and make money in the process.

Improves Mental, Physical, and Emotional Health

We all know the stress that comes with having one source of income. You lose focus and hope when you are unsure about your income. It can affect your relationships and turn you into a walking zombie and relying on one source of income alone is dangerous to your physical and mental health. You put in a lot of time to finish projects and please your boss, and other times you work overtime to finish pending work. You have no time to go to the gym or just relax. Many people complain about how overwhelming it is to have one source of income. You do everything possible to retain the job at the expense of your health. It also leads to mental health issues because you are always worried about things going wrong. You keep thinking: *What if I lose my job?* You become paranoid and lose focus. Your mental health starts to suffer, and before long, you cannot cope. It is in these ways, under these pressures and with these thoughts that depending on one source of income is dangerous to your mental, physical, and emotional health. You lack time to socialize with friends and family, and every time you *are* invited somewhere, you have no time for it.

Yet, despite its benefits, passive income requires commitment. You need to plan well to avoid mishaps and have everything that is needed to make passive income successful. You might not earn a lot of money, but at least you will be at peace.

Chapter 3: How to Make Money from Rental Property

It is no secret that you can make good money from rental properties. It goes without saying that a well-located real estate can generate good returns, more than covering the amount used to finance it. Those who have had single homes for a long time boast of large amounts of equity, and they have saved a lot of money over the years. For you to succeed in the real estate sector, you need to make smart decisions. Many people generate little returns because of making miscalculated decisions as their property ownership grows. It is easy to make money from your first rental property, and it is easy (and wise) to learn from the competition. Don't ignore competitors or write them off, as some of them have been in the sector for a long time. It is prudent to know your competitors and take time to learn from them; once you understand how the sector operates, you can proceed. Always use the best analysis tools to gauge the real estate market. Below are the secrets to making money using a rental property.

Budget Well

This is one area that most people go wrong: not budgeting well before buying a rental property. You must determine if you have the amount needed to buy the property, as well as determining if it is worth the investment and in good condition. You must ask these questions as you prepare the budget, ensuring that your calculations are correct. People make money in real estate by cutting their losses to increase profits. This means that you have to look for ways to increase profits by all means possible. It is good if you know all the risks linked to the rental property; you'll be in a better position to handle risks if you understand what they are. Use the experience of former real estate investors in your area and inquire how much is spent on properties in terms of expenses – both expected and unexpected, getting as much information as possible so that you are not caught off-guard. You can use a comparative analysis tool to get all the information needed, and that will also educate you more on other properties in a given area. You can use an investment property calculator to get the cost of buying a rental property. Have a realistic budget and expectations. There is no point of underestimating or overvaluing either the property or the costs needed to put it back into selling condition. Don't budget what you don't have; instead, plan with what you have. If you are waiting for the money from somewhere, wait until you have it. The budget-making process is sensitive. You can hire a financial expert to prepare the budget.

Know Your Competition

Some investors make the mistake of underestimating their competitors. On the contrary, you need to know them. Don't see your competitors as enemies, but people to learn from. If they have been in the industry longer, learn their secrets, if possible. The real estate sector is very competitive, and it is up to you to make a name for yourself. Firms try to outshine each other every day.

There are both long-term and short-term rentals. For you to succeed in the industry, you should know market trends. It informs you of customers' wants and areas to specialize in. Recently, baby boomers trended in selling their homes and shifting to apartments occupied by senior citizens. Landlords in this area observed the trend and learned where to invest. If a person made the mistake of buying a rental property to sell to baby boomers, then they would have incurred losses. Choose the correct rental strategy based on market trends and knowing your competitors will help you put things into perspective and enlighten you as to which areas to keep an eye on. Some people rush to join the real estate sector without understanding how it works. Analyzing your competition is the easiest way to learn how the market operates and also clarifies expectations. Additionally, you can learn from your competitors' mistakes and minimize risks. Competition is important because it keeps you on your toes. It also gives customers options to choose from. The real estate sector would be boring if there were only one firm or investors, and people would not be interested in investing in the sector. Competition is healthy and motivates people to work hard; real estate firms would not be putting extra effort if the customers did not have options! Customers are educated on quality and do not settle for less, so firms must offer quality goods and services to retain customers. Similarly, your rental property needs to match market expectations to perform well.

Give Customers Offers They Cannot Resist

Nothing attracts customers than good deals. When you offer quality services at a good price, customers are bound to come to your shop, and they will recommend your services to their family and friends. As an investor, buy a rental property that is in good shape at a reasonable price, and also consider the location. It needs to be appealing for the customers to develop interest.

Amenities make a huge difference as to why customers decide on your rental property. This is where market research comes in handy, informing you what customers are searching for. Once you determine what customers want, offer it to them. By doing this, you will have more people renting your property, avoiding the dry spells, like other owners. Dealing with a rental property needs smart people who can make good decisions, so learn the market and diversify your services, focusing primarily on what clients want and offering impeccable services. There are numerous rental properties, so make yours unique, make it stand out. You will get more people wanting to rent your property when you have all the amenities in place. Some people think that if they lower the price, they will not make good money, but that is not the case. Since clients are less likely to rent your property if it is expensive, it is better to lower the price somewhat and have renters, that to have no renters at all. Reduce your prices and maximize profits by keeping your properties rented.

Know and Abide by the Rules and Regulations

The real estate sector has rules and regulations, and failure to abide by them can lead to fines, or even your property being confiscated. You don't want that to happen after spending a lot of money to purchase it! Therefore, make it a point to know all the rules and abide by them for your own good. The first rule is knowing the laws and rental regulations in your area. Familiarizing yourself with the rules will save you stress along the way. Before you buy any property, find out whether you stand to gain or lose from it.

Rent to Good Tenants

The worst thing that can happen to a rental owner is to get a bad tenant. This is the kind of person who never pays rent on time, having to be reminded constantly to pay their bills. Such people are difficult to get along with and can drain your energy. If your property has shared amenities, such tenants make life difficult for others, as they often prioritize their needs at the expense of others. Getting rid of them is another nightmare. Even when you point out their mistakes, they never accept responsibility and instead, they become defensive. Getting good tenants is rare, so when you find the good ones (who pay their rent and bills on time, take good care of your property, and inform promptly when there are issues), *cherish them!* Some tenants cause drama with every small issue on your property, demanding rental refunds, while a good tenant calls and explains the issue in a civilized manner.

Ensure that the property is in good condition before you rent it. This will spare you the headache and complaints call from tenants. Any seasoned landlord can tell you that the secret to making a profit is getting good tenants. You want to get into the real estate sector with the right people, since horrible tenants can make you think twice about the venture; you may find yourself rethinking the entire plan and forfeiting everything just to escape the stress of bad tenants. Having good tenants is advantageous because you are convinced your property will be safe, saving you from endless repairs and complaints. Moreover, having good tenants will reduce managerial duties for you and make your life easy. There are some tenants that never allow the landlord to rest, always calling with a problem that needs urgent attention. A good tenant understands that you also need to rest. He/she understands that your life is not limited to meeting their demands. Also, a good tenant is patient with you, understanding those times when you cannot respond to demands immediately. A reasonable person should understand and give you time to address the issue. In such a scenario, a bad tenant will complain and threaten to leave. If such a tenant offers to leave, don't try to convince them to stay; let them go, as this will save you the trouble of their unrealistic demands. Having good tenants means that you get a good income every end month. They don't make excuses to avoid or delay paying rent, and because of their commitment, it is easy for you to understand if they face payment delays sometimes. Some tenants have the habit of delaying rent every month, always having an excuse. Dealing with such people can be a nightmare, and if you don't get rid of them, they will ruin your business. You can give a tenant a chance to correct his/her mistakes, but if they are not willing to change, look for a replacement. Bad tenants leave without notice, and a landlord will need to find a replacement before a tenant leaves to avoid having vacancies, as those vacancies represent missed income. A good tenant will provide plenty of advanced notice, giving you time to find a new renter, so do yourself a favor and review tenant applications before accepting them. It might take some time to go through all the applications, but it will save the stress. If you sense trouble, listen to your gut.

Hire a Property Manager

If you are able to afford it, hire a property manager. Some people have the money to invest in rental properties but lack the skills to manage it. A property manager ensures that your property makes a profit and runs smoothly, and you will not have to worry about things going wrong if you hire a manager; while it is an added cost, it saves you the trouble of dealing with rowdy tenants. Some landlords think they will lose a lot by hiring a property manager. However, this is a huge mistake because the chances of failure are high; it is highly unlikely that you will succeed the first time you try something. A property manager has experience and is best placed to maximize profits, and property management requires knowledge and skills. You need someone who will look for tenants to rent your property. You could do that alone, but there is no guarantee that you will succeed. Consult rental management firms for the way forward because, despite what many believe, hiring a property manager saves you money.

Choose a Good Location

Location is everything in a rental property. You may have a suitable property, but if the location is not ideal, tenants will not be interested. If the rental property is in the urban centers, it should be near the city centers where most people work. Where you invest is critical and determines whether you will make profits or not. You may find that you cannot invest where you live, finding a good rental property in another state. It is okay to invest elsewhere, provided the location is ideal. Location cannot be emphasized enough. Tenants want the easiest option, and while a landlord may have a nice property, if it is situated too far from their work area, tenants will be skeptical about renting it. Consider who the tenants will be; if the rental property is for single families, tailor it to meet their needs. If the property is for large families with kids, it should be near schools and hospitals and parks. Ensure the property has essential amenities for the tenants. Take time to analyze and choose an investment strategy, and refrain from choosing a rental property *just because it is available*. You do not know why people are not investing in it, but if you take the time to study the area, residents, and prospective tenants, you can choose properties that will make money. Making money from a rental property is easy if you follow the right steps and work hard. Consider the tenants' needs and strive to fulfill them; it's *all about the tenants*. When you have a property in a strategic location, you can refurbish it to appeal to clients.

Use Space Well

If you are a beginner, don't buy many rental properties at once. Use what you have, choosing carefully and acquiring the skills needed to manage big rental properties. You can start by renting your home, and you don't have to rent out your entire home. You can start by giving each tenant a room and grow from there. By doing this, you will save money, learn the trades, and make wiser investment decisions. There are numerous risks involved in rental property, hence the need to trade with caution. Avoid the urge to buy a rental property just because everyone is doing it. Establish goals and draft a plan on how to achieve it. Starting small is the surest way to rise up the ladder, plus you will not use a lot of money if you utilize your space well. Single people are the ones who can make this work. Instead of living in a three- or four-bedroom house alone, you can rent empty rooms. You will make money and learn what it takes to succeed as a real estate investor. Don't be fooled into thinking that you can make fast money in this sector; the ones who succeed are those that make smart decisions. You must be patient to grow. As a matter of fact, renting out single rooms can be more profitable for the entire house. Some investors start by renting separate rooms in their homes to gauge their performance. It is not that they lack the money, they want to develop skills. When they have acquired the necessary knowledge, they move to big rental properties. Chances of failure diminish when you start small.

Know the Value of the Rental Property

The first secret of making money from a rental property is to know its market value. Research the real estate market to know the rate charged by other landlords. Failure to know the rental value can lead to losses. Moreover, a high rate can scare the tenants away, so learn what works. You cannot overlook the importance of research in the real estate sector, as it will help you make the right decisions and minimize risks. Set a fair price to stay competitive in the market. When your rental property is in good condition and has a good rate, you will more tenants, but don't forget to ensure that it has all the amenities needed by your renters.

Improve Your Rental Property

Refurbish the rental property regularly. Tenants cannot live in a disorganized, broken, and dirty home. Use part of the money paid by tenants to make any needed repairs in the home. Consider painting the walls, repairing holes, cabinet doors, window latches, and all the small things. Improving your property allows you to charge more, and you will get profit more in the end. One of the reasons why some landlords do not repair properties is fear of spending more, but what they don't realize is that the tenants value efforts to maintain their homes; no one wants to live in a messy place. Even the landlord wants to live in a beautiful home. Landlords should put themselves in the tenants' shoes and maintain rental properties in such a way that they, themselves, would live in the home in its current condition.

Keep Tabs on Rental Expenses

Most investors make the mistake of spending a lot on rental upgrades and repairs, without considering the bottom line. While it is good to do repairs, it should not take all the profits. Don't underestimate operating expenses because they can bankrupt you! Maintenance and repairs can be difficult to track, but it must be done. A good tip is always to ensure that operating expenses are below the gross monthly income. Save money by cutting down on unnecessary expenses. If you want to decorate or add new features to your property, wait until you have the money. Services such as trash disposal and gardening are costly and can quickly eat away the profits. Drop some of the services or pass them to tenants; tenants will not mind paying extra if the services are crucial. Provide mandatory services and leave the rest to your tenants. You need to know where to draw the line. Some landlords have difficulty saying no to tenants requesting particular services (yard maintenance, for instance) just to find that the service eats up (or even exceeds) profits. Instead of saying yes to everything, ask for time to think about it; if the requests are costly, ask the tenants to chip in. The easiest way to get tenants' cooperation is to explain to them the importance of the service. Tenants may not know that they need a particular service until you explain it to them.

You can do some repair and maintenance work by yourself to cut costs. Some work done by professional contractors is not difficult, you only need to have the right equipment, and you are ready to go. Also, if you can get tenants by yourself, there is no need to hire a rental property manager. Know things that you can do to cut on expenses. Doing some of the work allows you to be actively involved in the management of the rental property, and you can manage the property if you have the time. What causes many to delegate duties is a lack of skills. Consult someone with experience and learn from them, as managing a rental property is not hard if you are willing to learn.

Offer Other Services

If others are only renting properties, you can expand your business by taking things a step higher. Customers are attracted to firms that put in the extra effort and offering additional services will not only attract customers but also increase income. You can offer services such as gym memberships, parking spaces, and internet services. The price should be reasonable so that many tenants can join. Many rental properties offer additional services to supplement monthly income. Making money as a beginner can be difficult because of vacant rooms. Additional services will help you during the dry seasons. Moreover, you can use money from services provided for repair and maintenance.

Chapter 4: Examples of Passive Income

There are several examples of passive income you can engage in. You are not limited to these examples. Before you engage in passive income, determine if it is the right one for you by understanding where your interests lie. Don't start a passive income because of what you can gain from it; the money may not always be there, and you may have to wait longer to see profits. If you were doing it for the wrong reasons, you would give up along the way. However, if you were genuinely interested in the venture, you will persevere through the challenges. These are just but examples to help you choose the right passive income.

Start a YouTube channel

Technology has changed how people interact. Gone are the days when advertisements were limited to television screens; you no longer have to watch TV to watch TV programs.

YouTube is a social media platform for content creators to interact with their followers. Content creators make money from the platform by marketing products and advertisements inside the video – or even outside the video viewing area on the user's screen.

Starting a YouTube channel is easy, and you can create a YouTube channel if you have a smartphone. While starting a channel is easy, maintaining takes effort. You need to connect with your followers and focus on what you love. Followers need to identify with you for them to subscribe to your channel. The more followers you have, the higher the income, but growing your channel may take some time. You will need another source of income as you grow your channel. Once you have a decent number of followers and start getting payments from YouTube, you can make it your main source of income. It is not a bed of roses; you are laying yourself bare to the whole world. Your life becomes public and can attract criticism, hatred, and jealousy. Some people have ended up closing their channels because of hate. Some followers send life-threatening texts to the content creators. It can be overwhelming and get out of control quickly, so you'll need to have thick skin to survive on the social media platform. People who have experienced success on the platform attribute it to hard work, diligence, and ignoring naysayers. It is not always easy to ignore harsh critics, so if you want to open a YouTube channel, keep the drawbacks in mind. The good side of this platform is that it allows you to explore your creative side, plus, of course, you can earn good money. Many content creators have started their companies and promote them through the platform. It requires dedication and self-discipline. If you are a student, plan your timetable in advance, i.e., you can upload one or two videos in a week, depending on your availability. Consistency is key if you want to make it on YouTube. Fans will appreciate your consistency in uploading videos every week, and regular uploads are the best way to grow your followers, AND it also increases your chances of getting partners!

Companies have changed how they advertise products. Customers are no longer moved by ads on TV; instead, testimonials are more appealing to them. Firms are collaborating with content creators to market their products at a fee. As a content creator, you need to have a high number of followers to appeal to companies, making your YouTube channel is a good source of income.

Another way to appeal to fans is to be unique. People talk about all sorts of things on the platform, but you should be authentic, and fans will identify with you. The truth is that not everyone can be successful on YouTube. Give it a shot if you have an interest in it. You can also collaborate with other YouTubers to reach more people. If your friend has many followers on the platform, you can reach out and do episodes for both channels. YouTube needs creativity, so don't upload videos just for the sake of uploading anything. Before you make any video, strive to connect to your followers.

YouTube is a good source of income because it can be done at any time, and you can do it anywhere you have a laptop/computer, a smartphone, and an internet connection. You can opt to shoot many videos for some months if you have a busy week ahead. Plan your calendar and prioritize the most important things, and don't forget to edit videos properly to appeal to viewers.

Invest in Real Estate

You can invest in real estate if you have the money. If you have an office that you have outgrown, you can rent or sell it. There is no point in letting a home sit empty while you can rent it to someone, or you might decide to sell it and make an instant profit. Others opt to rent because they might need it in the future. Whatever option you pick, make use of vacant properties. Also, you can buy a property and rent it out; consider buying older homes, renovating, and selling them (also called "flipping.") If you don't have enough money to buy a property, you can partner with someone, however, be careful who you choose to work with. A bad partner can dupe you, taking all your profits. Thus, it is better to wait — if you can — until you have all the money to join the real estate sector. However, if you find a nice property and fear losing it, you can work with a friend. Alternatively, you can request a loan from the bank.

Investing in real estate is lucrative, and you stand to gain a lot from joining the sector. It is important to note that returns may not come immediately. Some people have had to wait for a long period before they make profits. Therefore, be mentally prepared to wait to see returns. Also, be aware that the real estate sector may be somewhat flooded with too many homes and not enough renters; you may need to be unique and offer affordable rates. Be approachable, and practice listening; while buying or building a property, pay attention to market trends. Building without considering clients' expectations is counterintuitive. What clients think matters more than building a fancy apartment, and when a building meets the demands of tenants, making profits is a guarantee. Seek advice from experts before delving into the real estate industry.

Organic Farming

Farming is not easy-peasy, but it can yield good returns. People are slowly moving away from chemically-produced food products to organic ones. The number of organic farmers is low compared to market demands. Organic farming is sustainable as long as you have the right people, plus you can do it on your farm at home or hire an outside farm. Many people opt to buy farms, but whichever option you prefer, organic farming is taking the world by storm.

Many people are sick because of poor lifestyle (and food) choices. Doctors are advising patients to stay away from certain foods to stay healthy. The challenge for most people is the lack of money to sustain a healthy lifestyle. People have the notion that eating healthy is expensive, but that is debatable. Instead of buying fries and burgers every day, one could use the money to buy enough vegetables to last a week. Therefore, clean, and fresh food is affordable.

As an organic farmer, you must produce quality products to attract customers. You can lower the price slightly compared to the market rates. Selling quality products at a good price will increase profits. Moreover, you can buy another farm using profits. You can start small and increase when the demand for products increases. You can hire people to help if you have a large farm. The key is to avoid chemicals and only use organic ingredients.

Organic farming is a good source of income. You might spend a lot of money at first to buy seeds and hire help, but the returns outweigh the expenditure. A tip to making money from organic farming is monitoring expenses, keeping track of the amount used to pay laborers, buy equipment, and harvesting. Ensure that overall expenses do not surpass the gross income. Develop a good relationship with customers, and if you are the kind of person who finds it hard to interact with customers, consider hiring an expert.

Customers may need quality products, but they often value *the service more*. If you are rude and disregard customers' needs, they will leave. This sounds obvious, but some people are not suited to customer relations, and drive away their own income source! The solution to the problem is to ask for help if you find it hard to interact with clients and learning what customers in your area love and want. You cannot grow cassava when people in the area detest it. Grow foods that people love and buy often, and if you are unsure of what items to farm, ask residents what they like before you start farming. Organic farming is a sustainable venture and will earn you good money, as it already is transforming lives and creating wealth. Organic farming involves a lot of work, but the returns are worth it.

Lending Money

Lending money is a new way of making money, as some people dislike borrowing money from banks because of the high interest and are looking for alternative lending sources. This is where money lenders come in; you can lend money at a low-interest rate to attract customers. Keep in mind that many people have started this business, so be sure to make yours unique and appealing. If others lend up to a certain level, you can surpass it. If others have strict rules which prevent many from borrowing, you can have friendlier options for them.

However, money lending comes with a lot of challenges to keep in mind. Some people borrow, but they never return, so you must have a legal plan in place to follow them, as many change locations once they get the money. Moneylenders usually require borrowers to come with guarantors who will pay the money if the default. The guarantor acts as a collateral. However, some people are clever and bring people who cannot be traced, aiming to get the money and disappear. This is why money lending agencies have strict rules. It is not that they do not want to lend many people, instead, they fear lending money to the *wrong people*. If you decide to venture into this line of business, come up with strategies on how to address these challenges. Don't be too lenient because you will lose all the money; conversely, don't be super strict because you will scare away clients. To avoid losses, lend money to people you know and trust. You can start by lending to close friends and family members, setting friendly interest rates. Lending to family and friends can be tricky because some will never return the money, causing deep rifts. Someone once said that lending to family is like giving something and never expecting it back. Family members can bring down your business by defaulting to pay what they owe. Others will refuse to pay the interest, claiming that you cannot charge them. If you have such people in your family, don't lend them. Instead, look for trustworthy friends. When the business has grown, your friends can recommend their friends to you.

Lending money is tricky because you are not guaranteed profit, as defaults are common, and many lenders have given up along the way because of how stressful it is. If you become overwhelmed by having to follow your borrowers, try venturing into another business. Many people have experienced success in lending money. Don't let fear keep you from realizing success. Trust your intuition when someone asks for a loan. After doing a background check on someone, find out why they need the money. Some people borrow money that they can get easily from their family members or friends. Only lend money when someone gives valid reasons, and when you are sure of getting it back.

Car Wash

One of the fastest ways to earn money is to start a car wash. Nearly everyone has a car nowadays, and they all need to be cleaned regularly, so it's hard to go wrong with this business. A car wash is easy to start and maintain and, as an added benefit, you don't have to be there to make money, you can hire someone to do all the work. All you need to do is to get the right equipment, location, and workers. Finding an ideal spot is easy because cars are passing on streets all the time, everywhere. As there are numerous car wash businesses, you will need to appeal to customers by offering additional services such as carpet cleaning, Wi-Fi, or house-cleaning services. This is a nice way to supplement your income when the car wash business is down. Hire people who know how to relate to customers. Some employees do not know how to treat customers, failing to clean cars thoroughly and overcharging clients. The best way to ensure that customers get impeccable services when you are gone is to put someone in charge of employees. Hire someone who is reliable and trustworthy. His/her work will be to monitor the employees and collect the money. If you are a beginner, do the work yourself. This way, you will learn more about the business, and you will know the amount of money the business makes in a day.

One reasons why car wash businesses collapse is because the owners never took the time to study the business. You can spare a week to learn the business if you have other commitments. It is tempting to put someone in charge and focus on other things, but you may lose a lot in the process. There is no guarantee that the person you hire to monitor employees will hand in all the money. Other people have put surveillance cameras on the car wash premises to monitor employee movements. However, it is hard to put cameras in some areas. If you have a suitable location to put surveillance cameras, go ahead.

A car wash business needs commitment, and you must offer quality services to retain customers. If your business only offers shoddy work, your customers will quickly move on to another place, so invest in quality equipment, and you will not be disappointed. Sometimes employees are not to blame for poor services; if you do not buy quality equipment, services will always be poor. Another way to improve services is to maintain good employee relations by talking nicely to employees, paying them well. Complaints will be a thing of the past if you take care of employees. Increase their salaries when the profits increase. The best way to grow the business is to respect people that bring in the money. If you are in a position to do everything alone, do it and keep all the profits. If you aren't in that position, then hire great employees and treat them well. Making a car wash your passive income means you can make money while you sleep.

Rent Your Car

You can rent your car when you are not using it. There are many people who do not have cars and want to travel long distances. There are car lending companies that offer services to such people and you can get in touch with such companies and rent out your car. You can make more money if you have more than one car, and some people buy cars purposely to just rent them out. When people travel to other countries, they need cars to get around in. Car rentals has become popular over the years, so don't be left out of this new line of business!

Once your renter is finished using the car, you'll need to pick it up. One of the risks of this business is that sometimes your car may come back in bad condition, as others do not always know how to take care of other people's property — or care. You can ask for compensation if you spot any damage. However, sometimes the damage is hidden, only discovered after the renter is gone. This is why it is better to work with a car renting company who comes for your car, inspects that it is in good condition, and rechecks it when it is returned. You will part with a small fee, but your car will be in good condition when it is returned. You can make a good passive income depending on the condition of your car, and you stand to make decent money if you are in specific locations. For example, people hire cars regularly in urban centers compared to rural areas. Therefore, the car renting business makes more money in some areas than others.

Cleaning Services

You can make decent passive income from offering cleaning

services. Not everyone has a washing machine, some people are busy with work and don't have time to clean or take care of their homes. You can recruit two or three people to help you look for clients. If you have money, you can start a cleaning agency and advertise your business, and while the business will be slow at first, things will pick up with time. Offer quality services to keep clients. Many people are skeptical about seeking cleaning services because they fear it will not match their standards. If you are unsure about something, ask the client; don't assume that you know everything. Asking and being certain of your clients' expectations can save you time and energy. Find out what the clients want and *surpass their expectations*. Many people offer cleaning services, but there is a chance for you in the market if you tailor your services to clients' expectations. When given a chance to clean, keep in mind that this is a client, and clients talk. Remember, a satisfied client will always recommend you to a friend. The best way to improve your business is to meet the needs of clients.

List Your Home on Airbnb

You can make good money by simply listing your home on Airbnb, and if you own a house or apartment that you seldom use, it is about time you started making money from it. Airbnb is a company that rents homes to people around the world. Keep your house in good condition to increase the chances of your house being picked, because Airbnb lists homes on its websites (with pictures) and customers pick the ones that they like. However, listing your home on the platform comes with challenges you need to keep in mind. Some people have complained in the past of not getting paid after renting their homes, and some clients damage things in the house. While you can get good money from listing your home on Airbnb, keep the risks in mind. Address the risks by only renting your home to trustworthy people, doing a background check on prospective clients before handing out the keys. Moreover, don't let strangers stay in your home for too long. Staying more than a month is not ideal because they may leave your place in disarray. If you are uncomfortable with the client's demands, speak up. All that in mind, people are becoming wealthy overnight by listing their homes on Airbnb.

Chapter 5: Online Business Ideas and How to Profit from Them

There are countless online business ideas you can try. Thanks to technology, you don't have to go to the office to earn money. On the contrary, many people are creating wealth in the comfort of their bedrooms, dens, and kitchens. Online businesses are versatile and flexible, giving you control over your time. The key to creating wealth from an online business is choosing the right business, and many people make the mistake of starting an online business because others are doing it. They see other people's success and assume that it is the right thing for them to do. This is the wrong approach and may lead to frustration, so before you embark on starting an online business, conduct research to determine if it is the right one. Foremost, do something that you enjoy. While online businesses are fairly easy, it might take a while before you make any profit, so patience is key when having such a business. Also, be ready for unpleasant remarks from critics. Despite its challenges, you can make a fortune by starting an online business. Below are some online business ideas you might consider.

Start a Blog

Starting a blog is now easier than ever! Starting a blog and monetizing it take commitment, as you don't just post content once a month and expect to make money out of it. You must post good content regularly to attract a huge following. Once you have a large number of followers, you can approach retail companies with a good offer. As mentioned above, brands are moving away from the traditional style of advertising, as customers no longer rely on ads they see on TV. Instead, they are more attracted to testimonials, which means that brands are collaborating with bloggers to market their products. Getting firms to work with is not as easy as most people think, and it can take years before one gets a nod from a brand. As a blogger, you have to convince the brand that you have influence with your many followers, guaranteeing returns on their investment. Brands have a way of gauging your influence over your followers. Your followers can be given a code to use to buy products at the company. They use the code to determine the number of people you have influenced to shop at the brand. Making money from blogging is not easy; you will only see results if you have a strong relationship with your followers, and you can do this by establishing that strong connection by answering their questions and considering their ideas. Some bloggers have giveaways to show appreciation to their followers. Interacting with your followers helps you to know the kind of content to make, and some bloggers lose followers due to a lack of interaction (you can hire someone to respond to questions to increase the number of followers!) Another reason why bloggers find it hard to make money is because of low price quotes to companies. You must know your worth as a blogger, and not undervalue yourself, setting the price and sticking to it. It is okay to negotiate, but don't go for the first offer.

Blogging is an ideal source of passive income. Creativity will earn you good money from blogging, but many bloggers make the mistake of copying what others are doing. Instead of following the majority, be creative. Find intriguing, yet unique topics to discuss and encourage your followers to comment and share your content. It may take a while before you make money from blogging, and while you may not make a lot of money at first, blogging is good for anyone thinking of starting an online business. As an added benefit, it a nice way to improve your language, because writing and reading books is the oldest trick to improving grammar. You will kill two birds with one stone - earn money and polish your vocabulary.

Affiliate Marketing

You can promote someone's products and earn a commission in the process; this is called "affiliate marketing." People do affiliate marketing by promoting products such as websites, eBooks, and products, and the number of people publishing content has increased dramatically. Entrants need people to market their content to increase the number of followers. You stand to make a lot of money doing affiliate marketing, but to get clients, you need to advertise your services, convincing clients that you will do a good job. Many people shop online, and firms are competing for customers, so you must remember that, like a regular job, you must do everything to please the client. Going the extra mile will not only earn you more clients but also build your reputation.

Before you launch a marketing campaign, take time to understand what the client wants. While you can make suggestions on how to convey the message, the client makes the final decision. Stay on top of your game by consulting other affiliate marketers, learning what makes them unique and how to improve your game. Affiliate marketing is ever-changing and requires someone who is willing to learn, as new technologies come out every day and need someone who is alert and willing to learn and apply such information.

A happy client means more income. If you are a beginner, take time to learn how affiliate marketing is done; rushing to get started will lead to silly mistakes, so watch tutorials online or consult an expert. Not everyone is willing to share their secrets to success, but if you keep looking, you will find someone willing to help. Affiliate marketing is a credible source of income and many people are providing for their families using affiliate marketing.

Publish eBooks

It is true that technology has changed everything. Gone are the days when people had to buy books. Today books are published online for readers, making it easier and much more convenient for the writer who no longer have to find publishing houses to publish and sell their books. All they need to do is publish books online, and readers will find them. Also, eBooks are easy to write (especially nonfiction) because all the information is already on the Internet; the author just has to find and compile it.

Creativity is vital when writing eBooks. It does not entail copying information from a certain source and pasting it. There are tools used to check plagiarism, so you must be cautious. Be unique, witty, and funny. You can earn a living off publishing eBooks. The more books you write, the more money you make; you can even hire writers to assist you and increase profits. You can market your books on Amazon or collaborate with affiliate marketers.

Sell Your Brand

If you are having a difficult time finding the right person to market your products, do it yourself. You can use a lot of tips and tricks online to become polished and well-marketed. Selling your product is advantageous because you get to focus on what you want. Delegating the duty to someone else might not do justice to your brand because they don't understand it like you do. Someone else might do things in a hurry so they can focus on other brands. Therefore, selling your own brand is the best way to ensure that the correct information is provided to the consumer, plus self-selling keeps you in touch with the brand. Some brand owners don't know what their brands represent because they delegate so much work that they lose touch with what they own. Losing touch with your brand means you lose touch with clients; you cannot talk authoritatively about your products. On the other hand, selling your brand saves you money, enabling you to form a connection with clients through interaction.

Create an App

There are so many apps for smartphones, tablets, and PCs on today's market, making it hard to keep up with, as it seems every day a new app is created to solve a problem. There are apps to help people watch their weight, track water consumption, measure distance, watch the stars… and the list goes on. Even so, companies are approaching app creators to make unique and appealing apps, and as the creator is basically the only cost in app creation, advertising is the only other cost. In addition, learning how to create apps is easy thanks to online tutorials, and many young people make a living off apps. Because the market is competitive, you have to convince clients to give you work, showing them that you can do a good job. The best way to convince clients about your capabilities is to show them what you have created before. If you are a beginner, learn from other developers because watching tutorials alone is not enough. You can enroll in a class or consult an expert. Technology changes every day, and as a developer, you must move along with it.

App development is a good source of passive income; however, it involves a lot of work and needs commitment. Smartphones are everywhere, the market is lucrative, and getting an interested buyer is almost guaranteed if you never assume that you know everything, observing market trends, and listening to clients. Offer to advise as an expert but leave the final decision to the client; otherwise, you may offend your client (who is not interested in having your ideas shoved down their throats!) Apps that perform well in the market generate thousands in revenue for the creators. You make money from advertisements, making this a great source of income to supplement your other earnings.

Consultancy Services

Becoming a social media consultant is a good strategy to make money online. Firms seek services from social media consultants on how to promote their products online. To become an online consultant, familiarize yourself with different social media platforms. Learn how they can be used to market businesses and products, and once you have the knowledge, approach brands, making offers they cannot refuse. (It helps if you have a big number of followers.) You also need to show them that you are a professional, because companies must be sure that you will deliver. There are tons of consultancy services online; take time to learn how your competition does the work and goes about their business.

A secret to getting clients is focusing on improving their image. Brands seek such services because they are stuck or want an expert opinion. When you venture into this field, you have to look at things with a critical eye, but not afraid to voice your ideas. Clients may not like it when you don't accept their views, but they will appreciate your honesty. For one to offer impeccable services, he/she needs to conduct market research, learning the trends and what customers expect. Offering consultancy services is the surest way to increase your income.

Business Consultants

If you have been in an industry for a long time, you can share your knowledge for a fee. There are many small business owners scouting for knowledge, and they all search online for the needed information. So, you can start a social media page specifically for business consultancy services. Not many have ventured into this field, thereby making it a profitable source of passive income.

You can arrange for one-on-one meetings or hold meetings online but be sure to ask each client how they prefer to meet up. Businesses collapse due to a lack of knowledge, but as an expert, you can help struggling businesses rise through the ranks. Some consultants have expanded, adding other trusted consultants to their firm, and eventually becoming big consulting companies.

Start an Online Store

We all have a friend who loves to shop online (and we may be that friend!) If someone said that you could shop at the comfort of your sofa or kitchen chair two decades ago, you would not have believed them. But today, you can buy a range of items (from clothes to tools to furniture) online, having them delivered right to your door. There are many online stores, and everyone wants to tap into the market. Starting an online store is convenient because you will not use the money to rent and decorate a physical store, often referred to as "brick and mortar." Moreover, you can save money by running it yourself, compared to traditional stores where you need to hire workers.

To maximize profits, hire affiliate marketers to promote your brand. In addition, have quality clothes that appeal to a wide range of customers. Operating an online store is made easier by using a delivery company to ship customers' orders; be sure to work with a delivery firm that operates worldwide. Another added advantage with online stores is you gain customers worldwide because once you create a page on any social media network, everyone can see it. This generates traffic on your page. Customers become frustrated when they don't receive their orders on time.

Setting reasonable prices, being aware of scammers, and waiting until you receive full payment for items before delivering are ways to thrive in your online store. Starting an online store is simple, saving time and energy as compared to brick-and-mortar stores. It saves you from the trouble of repairing and maintaining the store. Client-seller interactions also create opportunities for the business to expand.

Start a YouTube Channel

Make good money easily by starting a YouTube channel. People are on online to find people that they can relate to, and if a subject is appealing to you, you can start a channel and talk about it; others will find you! The good thing with starting a YouTube channel is that you will not spend money to start or run the channel. Moreover, you will meet and interact with people from different backgrounds. The best way to build a connection with followers is to focus on impacting *lives* instead of money. While there is nothing wrong with wanting money out of, it is not sustainable. There will be days when you will not feel like creating content, and times when you lack motivation, yet the deadline is near. During tough moments, passion is what keeps you going. If you started creating content for the sake of money alone, it would not last. Instead, focus on sharing meaningful content, and money will follow. When people see that you are passionate about helping others, they will automatically subscribe to your channel. Moreover, they will share your videos which will help grow your channel. Stay away from drama as much as possible. It is easy to be caught up in the glamour and fame that YouTube brings, but remember to stay grounded. Stay true to who you are when you become successful. There are YouTube celebrities who change once they become famous and successful.

Advertising

You can advertise products, websites, and people online. You can also advertise films on your social media page. To influence many people, you need to have many followers. Moreover, you also need to be an opinion leader. While many brands opt to work with celebrities to advertise their products, not everyone is a celebrity, and the world gets that. However, you need to convince the brand you wish to work with that you can do a perfect job, and that you can advertise brands on Facebook, Twitter, or Instagram.

One of the great things about advertising is that you can do it anytime. As long as you meet customer's expectations, you are free to focus on other things. Moreover, you can ask someone for help, and you get better results when you have multiple people advertising the same product. When companies create ads, they send them to numerous media outlets in order to have a wide reach to increase the chances of success. In a similar manner, recruit people to help you advertise brands.

Don't forget to sign an agreement with the client before starting the work.

Online Baking

The great thing about the internet is that passion can be turned into a source of income easily. If you are passionate about baking, but lack resources and location to start, the internet is the solution, as there are thousands of people offering a wide range of services online, and you can become one of them! Moreover, some of them make more profits than those with physical stores! People have moved their services online in attempts to cope with the changing times because, in today's world, having a shop is not enough to attract and retain customers. The best combination is having a physical store AND promoting your services online, and in this way, more people hear about your services. Start a baking class online and earn money from it by explaining to viewers your specialty, and why they should consider joining your class and not others'. There are many bakers online, and all of them are scrambling for clients, so you must be unique to get clients. You can recruit people to help when the number of followers increases. Many bakers have grown their businesses beyond expectations.

Become a Foreign Language Teacher

Many people across the world are interested in learning foreign languages. Some do it for educational purposes, others do it for fun, and others do it for job reasons. Being a foreign language teacher has many perks. You get to interact with people from different backgrounds, sharing the knowledge you already have, thereby making it the easiest thing in the world. There is no research or resources used to start teaching; all you have to do is start a social media page and advertise your services.

We all know that the most effective way to learn a new language is to interact with native speakers. Therefore, as a native speaker, you have an added advantage over someone who learned the language secondhand. If you are a native speaker, then you are missing out on a chance to make money! Becoming a foreign language teacher is not complex and can be done through Skype or Hangouts. You can start with one client and see how it goes. Some people have had success, teaching ten or more people during one session.

The key to attracting clients is to be polite. This a communication class; you should show that you are good at it. Apart from being a native speaker, you need to carry yourself in a respectful manner!

Sell Online Courses

Several companies hire people to sell their courses to students. If you have the expertise, you can make good money doing this, but you'll need to be on numerous social media platforms to reach many people, and learn about each course that you are selling so you aren't caught off guard by student questions. You can sell courses online at any time and make good money from it, but also, you can teach online courses if you have the knowledge to do so. There are many professors online teaching students and earning good money, however, they were not an overnight success. Patience is important as you will wait for some time before you start earning. Still, selling online courses is a simple and viable source of income.

Chapter 6: Why Some People Find It Easier to Create Multiple Streams of Income Than Others

If you have multiple streams of income, it means you have diversified your investment portfolio. The truth of the matter is that everyone wants to enjoy financial freedom without constraints. While most millionaires (who have five or more streams of income) have known this secret, the majority of the population still struggles with having more than one stream of income. Remember, when one stream of income suffers loss, then the others can make up for the damage without so much suffering and drama. When none of the streams are down, you are making tons of money; when one is down, you'll hardly notice!

Relying on employment alone may not provide the financial freedom some require, and many try a side hustle to supplement the income from their regular job. If you are not business-oriented, then you can still use your talent and passion to generate revenue. Financial independence requires hard work and needs a lot of dedication; this means that the faint-hearted may give up along the way, especially if things do not go as well as expected.

You can find multiple streams of income from the same line of business or different lines altogether. It entirely depends on the level of involvement, the total time you have to dedicate to both streams and both sets of target customers. Having multiple streams of income in the same business is more manageable in terms of management. For instance, if you are a blogger, you can consider doing content creation on the side, making and selling digital courses, writing eBooks, and selling on Amazon, as well as becoming an affiliate marketer. You will be doing different things from the same platform, with all payments coming to you differently;

this is far much better than blogging alone, which would have provided you with only one income.

The ways mentioned above are not the routes from which to earn from blogging. You can do consulting, you can run ads in your blogs and make money from ad revenue, and you can also have a podcast in the same blog. How cool is that? Starting an entirely different business from the one you already have may require more income and thorough market research. Also, consider whether you have enough time to dedicate to both. If not, one may suffer and eventually collapse; this doesn't mean that you cannot do both. An optimal way to try this: commit a lot of time to one side of the business until it can sustain itself, requiring little time or attention from you. At this point, starting another business will be realistic because the other firm is up and running and sustaining itself.

These discussions lead us to the one argument that often comes up: Why do some people find it easier to create a lot of streams of income than others? For the rest of this chapter, we are going to discuss this issue in depth, providing you with insights that can make you resilient and give you the drive to create your additional streams of income. It's never too late to start, and as long as you are mentally and emotionally ready to endure whatever outcome, be it positive or negative, you are good to go.

Some people love the idea of passive income. Passive income is the money earned without trading time for dollars. People who have exploited this and become successful enjoy ultimate financial freedom. Most social media influencers do this, as well as many Millennials who have found it very rewarding, making use of all of the available technology. For example, once you write an eBook and post it on Amazon, you can make money on the same book for years and years. The same thing applies to make digital courses, offering them online, and also blogging about them while making money on affiliate sales from advertised products (if a student customer clicks on it and purchases it.) With the internet, your possibilities are almost unlimited!

Passive income may not offer you millions of dollars in a year, but it can provide you with some extra money to cover expenses – especially those emergencies that crop up. The best thing with passive income is that once you get a stream "flowing", seldom do you have to spend a lot of time on it, you simply sit back and wait for the returns.

Sadly, some people assume they can start a stream without becoming involved with the process at all, while others understand (and remain aware) that the passive income they are creating requires deep involvement and dedication on the outset. Others merely do it as a survival technique when they fear potential financial strain. With time, however, passive income may turn out to be a great wealth creation strategy, generating income for decades.

Those successful multi-stream income producers have been able to quit their 8-5 job to do their own thing and are passionate about it. Such people claim to be more satisfied in their choices and with time, they have found themselves making more money than they ever expected! There are also other people who, over time, have developed dependency syndrome, relying so much on their 9-5 job that they live hand-to-mouth. Every penny of their income is used to pay bills and buy food, leaving them nothing for savings.

For this reason, they have a constant fear of what will happen to them if they resign from their jobs. While they may have an idea for a business they want to try, they lack the money to fund their ideas. Some forget to consider what might happen if their company decides to eliminate their jobs; this means they will have no income to sustain them until they find another position. Before you find yourself in this position, start discovering the things that you can do during weekends or when you aren't working, things that can bring in an extra income. It can be fitness, cooking, gymnastics or becoming a singing coach. You might offer cleaning services, lawn mowing, landscaping; anything that you enjoy doing and do well, consider offering it to others during non-working times. With persistence, you can generate enough money to start your own business, breaking the yoke of employment income as an only source of income.

Many people have missed the fact that the nature of work is changing, holding on to the concept of earning from employment alone. Others have embraced the idea of working from home and diversifying their income while sitting at the kitchen table, or the desk in the extra bedroom. They are not afraid to take risks and explore additional income options, believing that income from different sources poses fewer financial risks, which in turn gives them more control in their financial situation. They understand that multiple streams create the most income, *exponentially* more compared to income from only one source.

These entrepreneurs embrace globalization and technology, using it for their advantage. They already understand that if they don't, they will be taken over by intelligent technologies that get introduced every year. They, therefore, strive for multiple streams of income to act as protection when they face emergencies like job loss or health crises. *They plan so as not to fail.* If something throws their income for a loop, they have a backup plan that can protect them.

Sadly, others who do not yet to embrace these ideas are putting all their eggs in one basket, creating more risk during emergent times.

People who create multiple streams of income work very hard. If they are still employed, they understand that quitting a job to start generating a variety income streams might be a good idea, but it takes preparation. Making the extra effort, they use the spare time they have (and savings or income from their job) to generate more than one stream of income. This explains why people in the same job rank and same salary scale do not enjoy the same living standards. Some take their spare time to create an environment for success in terms of multiple streams of income; *they make it happen.*

If one puts in a lot of effort in whatever they do, eventually, it will pay off. You can be a real estate agent and schedule a meeting with your potential clients on your day off. By doing this, you will still earn money from your job and commissions from a successful deal. You can also be a broker or real estate consultant and connect clients to the best properties as well as link them to the kind of agent they require. Of course, you will work extra hard to achieve all this, but at the end of the day, it will be worth it. Also, note that those who work hard should also work *smart;* this means that the strategies that you adopt should be useful and reasonable. If you do not strategize well, then your hard work may never pay off. Always consider interacting with people in the same line of business who have gained more experience than you over the years; listen to their stories and learn from their experience.

During planning for anything, goals are of utmost importance. People who find it easy to build multiple income streams will intentionally focus on the most specific goals. They draft goals they intend to achieve, focusing on exactly how they will reach those goals, and they consider different outcomes. They remember that goals must be SMART. This acronym stands for Specific, Measurable, Attainable, Relevant, and Time-bound. Only be reaching these goals can they meet their objectives.

The exciting part about such people: when they do not achieve their goals, they do not leave; instead, they evaluate themselves, discover the things they did wrong, and come up with ways to avoid the pitfalls they suffered the first time around. In simple terms, they learn from their mistakes. To them, failure is a learning experience that shapes someone, and not the end of the journey.

Also, if things do work out, they don't stop there, either. They come up with a better strategy to yield even more income than their first game plan. In simple terms, they use the money to make money.

Failure and success do not scare them, as they understand that both can motivate them in different ways. As they keep developing additional streams of income from the successful ones, they keep growing and growing, increasing their income and seizing all opportunities that come their way.

Patience is a virtue, not just to everyone but also to people who intend to build multiple streams of income. People who have mastered the plan o to develop multiple streams of income knows this and understand that creating numerous streams of income is not a get-rich-quick scheme. You need to be patient with everything, or else you can find yourself in debt. It takes a lot of time, and sometimes your patience can be tested. For example, real estate rentals (or flipping) offers multiple streams of income, but to realize them, you must save for some years so that you do not start your investment in debt. After saving, you can buy a house, renovate, and sell at a higher price. Alternatively, you can rent out the house or use it to host guests (Airbnb) as well as functions. The rental income can be an excellent passive income as you do other things.

You can also use the profits to purchase additional rental properties. doubling or tripling your income stream. With patience over the years, you can increase your real estate holdings until you have the income you've dreamed about. As you plan to save, consider other passive income ideas to increase your monthly savings, getting you closer to your dream. Patience cannot be understated, and it is a habit that can be learned by all.

We believe that now you know why some people find it easy to create additional streams of income. We can now point out some of the reasons why other people still find it hard to come up with more streams of income for the remaining part of this chapter.

Job Security

There is a traditional mindset that has been passed from one generation to the next over the years: once you are an adult, you need to wake up early, go to work, climb the corporate ladder, save for retirement and then enjoy your pension in your old age. For those without education or job skills, they were delegated to home service jobs (i.e., maids) or other menial labor. Technology is changing this mindset because of the rapid incorporation of modern technology in the workplace, even leading to a reduction of the workforce. Some people still find themselves stuck in a job with a good pension plan or permanent positions, whether they pay well or not.

The comfort of having a situation where they can't lose their jobs gives them a feeling of job security. Perhaps they won't see the need for creating an additional income because they feel that once they retire (or face terminal illness) they will have savings to cover those circumstances. They feel safe where they are, having access to savings and government services at no cost.

Fear of Taking Risks

Most of the time, young people find it easy to take a risk when they are younger. As one gets older, then the fear of taking a risk takes its toll, and often people see others taking years to recover from significant losses or failures. Others have many needs that require their attention, like family obligations, so as they grow old, the fear of failure often looms at the back of their minds.

If things do not work as expected, not only will they suffer, but their children as well. They, therefore, do not see failure as a learning experience but as a downfall that they should avoid at all costs.

You can take risks at any point in your life — it does not matter how young or old you are. People realize financial freedom at different times in their lives. Risk is risk; it does not choose the time or only affect certain age groups. Those who fear failure should seek support from family or friends, knowing that there are people to turn when things do not go as expected. These are the same people they will likely celebrate with when things go well!

Social Security

In the United States, Social Security benefits kick in when one reaches a particular age, making it possible for most to pay their bills and providing some with a safety net when they stop working. Knowing this exists, some people relax and only focus on earning money that sustains them at the present moment, failing to realize that this government system might fail, or that they income coming may not be enough to sustain their needs once they reach that age of retirement. They fail to realize that they may not enjoy the same financial safety that their grandparents enjoyed.

Many millennials are striving for financial security by creating more streams of income, realizing that if they don't qualify for social security in their old age, they will survive on their profits. Social Security has a lot of conditions attached to it, and some people opt to either wait until the full age of 68 to apply — or opt not apply at all. It is essential to work on creating another stream of income and save so that if social security is not there by the year 2035, you can still lead a meaningful, productive life.

Debts and Loans

It is sometimes tough to make long term plans if you can barely make plans for the next day or week. Some people find themselves in debt from student loans, mortgages, and healthcare. In this circumstance, most income is used to pay back the debts, leaving them with no remaining income to save or use for investing in other streams of income. This leave them financially drained and not able to tell how they can achieve the desired financial freedom. Additionally, if they fail to repay the debts as expected, they may have to pay additional charges that they did not expect.

If you find yourself in this situation, consider a side hustle to generate income to pay back your debts. Once you settle all debts, then consider starting an additional stream of income and start putting money in savings to help cover emergency situations and also to find additional streams of passive income. Consider setting up an online business that does not require a lot of upfront capital to set up (i.e., blogging.)

Based on all the discussions above, it is true that additional streams of income are the key when generating wealth and realizing financial freedom. If you find yourself unable to build more than two streams of income, then you need to re-evaluate yourself. It is something that everyone can do as long as they set out purposefully to do so, being psychologically prepared for the best and worst. Do not quit your job before your side hustle starts generating income, and if possible, create two or more income streams that are self-sustainable before leaving your job. Be wise in how you strategize and plan for everything. Most people prepare for success and not a possible failure. The same way you plan for your success is the same way you need to plan for failure; that way, you can learn from both. Also, consider venturing in a side hustle you are passionate about; that way, you will get the personal satisfaction that comes from multiple successful streams of income.

Chapter 7: How to Sustain Multiple Streams of Income

Diversifying your earnings through multiple income streams is important because if one source fails to bring in money, you still have other profitable sources to keep you afloat. If your only source of income is from formal employment, you're exposing yourself to a very big risk, as you can lose your job at any time, without notice, leaving you with no source of income. Building multiple sources of income protects you from financial risks.

When you have many income streams, you will be in a position to build additional income, allowing you to exercise better control over your money affairs than when earning income from one source. The workplace is facing rapid changes due to globalization, technology, and other factors that you have no control over. As the years go by, intelligent technology continues to advance, meaning that demand for manual labor will continue decreasing. If you want to be on the safe financial side, you will have to consider the idea of multiple streams of income.

It's a fact that when you have many sources of sustainable income, you have more stability during a health crisis, job loss, downturn, or any other emergency that may crop up. Average millionaires have at least seven income streams or more; they understand risks that come with putting all their eggs in one basket. One income source will never be as profitable as from different income sources. Multiple income streams are more effective when most of them are *passive* income streams.

In the olden days, running multiple streams of income was time-consuming, expensive, and difficult. Fortunately, this situation has changed with the invention of the internet; creating and sustaining multiple sources of income has become more affordable, faster, and easier.

Multiple streams of income are very different from one another; some will require you to put in some energy and time to keep them running, while others are passive. Multiple streams of income play a key role in boosting your income and giving you a chance to do other things that can still earn you extra money. There are many avenues that you can pursue, including online courses, e-commerce stores, YouTube marketing, blogging, affiliate marketing, etc.

In the past, there were very few options available for making money other than formal employment. Presently, there are thousands of things that you can involve yourself in attaining your financial goals. You can opt for the simplest of things, such as online freelancing and flipping real estate. Choosing your multiple streams of income depends on several factors, such as your expertise, lifestyle, and goals. Let's look at the many modern avenues that you can use to earn the extra income that you need.

If you intend to create multiple streams of income, you must observe proven avenues that will increase your chances of success. Start by singling out one income stream that you have an interest in or consider similar ideas. It could be real estate, online businesses, digital marketing, etc. The first income stream that you create must be something you are passionate about; otherwise, you will soon lose interest, which can stall the income stream.

When setting up the first income stream, it could be difficult because you have no experience in running it. You are mainly relying on the information you have come across on the internet or by word of mouth. You may need to come up with a support team, overcome hurdles to success, and create adequate cash flow to keep your income stream running. The first income stream must be something that you can pursue even in the *absence of funds*.

How Can You Sustain Multiple Streams of Income?

Building multiple streams of income is not as hard as many people think; there is easy access to opportunities, information, and people. Some people think that for them to create multiple streams of income, they need to have a full-blown existing business, but this is not true. Building sustainable multiple streams of income come down to practicing the following:

- Understanding that by creating a new income stream, you're laying a foundation for your long-term benefits
- Using what you are good at to your advantage
- Explaining to people about your intentions
- Being creative
- Taking action

There are thousands of articles on the internet that give insight into avenues that you can explore to earn more money. Human beings have different capabilities and passions; what works for one individual may not work for you.

Laying the Foundation

Schemes that promise you recipes for getting rich overnight are unrealistic and unattainable. Building successful and sustainable income streams needs strong foundations, and patience and self-awareness are crucial in creating those solid foundations. An income stream could be earning you only %5 in the beginning; if you have a long-term vision and patience, it can grow and earn you many times more. Small earnings when the stream is new should not discourage you. Give it time.

Using What You Are Good at to Your Advantage

We all have diverse interests; if your interest lies in a certain field and you can offer value to another person from the same, then you can earn money. People tend to take a keen interest in what others are engaging in and copy them; this may only work for a short time, not for the long-term. You will always come across ads about how people have made hundreds of dollars from certain avenues; pass those by. The best way to achieve higher success rates is by focusing on what you are already good at, which will make it very easy to run your new stream. A simple example is earning money by participating in online surveys; you give your opinion and get paid.

Explaining to People about Your Intentions

You will be more successful if you write down your vision and goals and keep track of them. The chances of your income stream succeeding increase when you have accountability partners. Telling people about your dreams and goals may feel like it decreases the probability of succeeding, possibly making your overconfident (since you feel like you have already done what you are describing.) Verbalizing and visualizing your goals — and being accountable to those you have told – helps bring you back to reality when you've drifted away from those goals.

Being Creative

There are very many creative ways in which you can build multiple sustainable streams of income, namely:

- Selling eBooks
- Freelancing on Microsoft Excel jobs
- Nutrition and fitness coaching
-

- Providing loans for others
- Investing in real estate
- Affiliate marketing

Taking Action

If you fail to act, none of the above will hold any weight. Even if you fail after taking action, you will have learned something that you can use for future trials. To create sustainable and successful streams of income, always invest in an idea that you are passionate about, one that you can keep going, even with no income.

Tips for Creating Multiple Streams of Income

Given that there are a few setbacks of having multiple streams of income, the advantages outweigh the risks, especially if you are building additional streams generated in a home business. The following are steps that can help you to build more streams of income from your existing home business:

Set Realistic and Achievable Income Goals

One of the most important things that you must do when building multiple streams of income is setting goals. You must align your financial decisions with your needs. If you are planning or thinking of ways to make extra income, you need to ask yourself: What do I intend to achieve from this investment? How much money am I expecting to make from this source of income? Setting income goals can make it easier for you in planning. You can come up with long-term or short-term goals, but most importantly, set targets.

Research on the Available and Most Viable Options

Before investing in multiple streams of income, research the available options; this plays a crucial part as you engage and develop additional income streams. The research will give you clear insights about possible avenues, as well as what you can expect from the same. By doing proper research, you will understand what can work for you or not; you will have an idea of how hard you will need to work as well as the capital you will need to start a stream of income. Research is mandatory.

Testing the Waters

Not every income-generating hustle or stream is easy for everyone; it depends on your expertise and how much you are ready to sacrifice for your stream of income to be successful. In some instances, the only way you can find out if a stream will work in your favor or not will be by immersing yourself in it and finding out for yourself. You can start your streams of income while still being employed elsewhere; this gives you the chance to explore before settling down on three, four, or more income streams.

Remember that Failing is a Possibility

There isn't any guarantee that your streams of income will be sustainable or successful; you have to be open to the possibility of failure. It's only through trying that you will know the outcome, so always be realistic; you may have to keep trying before hitting the jackpot.

Points to Remember When Creating Sustainable Multiple Streams of Income

- Decide and set up a *single stream of income at a time*. Setting up of new income streams can be time-consuming and tedious, so avoid starting many streams of income with the hope of becoming a millionaire overnight. You will end up directing your focus to different areas at the same time, thinning your effect overall, and slowing you down in the end. Make it your goal to have tools, schedules, and systems in place; these will assist you in creating other income streams down the road.

- Give the additional streams of income the effort and time they require to keep them running; once the income starts trickling in, you can think of starting other streams of income. However, if the new stream fails to bring in any income, give it some time before deciding to abandon it. It may just need a tweak or two to get things flowing.

- Creating new streams of income can be time-consuming, however, if you choose to create a new stream within an existing business, it can be easier and faster. The size of the existing business isn't a determining factor when starting a new stream of income within the same business. For instance, when Amazon.com was taking off, they were selling books. Presently, Amazon.com sells a huge variation of products, as well as media streaming and business services.

- Many entrepreneurs who own service companies also add books and coaching to their existing income streams. Bloggers doing affiliate marketing can write their courses and books to link to their existing income stream.

Advantages of Having Multiple Stream of Income

In addition to making extra income, there are many other reasons why you should consider having multiple streams of income, namely:

- Creating many income-generating streams is easier than building a single stream, i.e., it's easier to earn $1500 from four streams of income than earning $3000 from a single stream.

- Multiple streams of income help in reducing the possibility of having no income, if a single stream of comes to a halt for whatever reason, you still have other streams that will sustain you. If you have home businesses, multiple streams of income can help you to offset your bills.

- It keeps you busy, as you will most probably be doing different tasks to keep each stream running at any given time.

- Job security; with the emergence of Artificial Intelligence, companies are downsizing on the number of their employees. Other companies have had to close down due to financial difficulties, rendering many people jobless. You can cushion yourself against this risk by building secure and viable means of livelihood from your home. You can tap into various markets by creating several sources of income.

- Unique opportunities: you can follow your dreams and passions, creating streams in an area that interests you. Having one source of income isn't realistic these days, especially with the cost of living being very high. The internet offers many possibilities; you can build viable online businesses and make use of your interests and skills. Whether it's finance, writing, marketing, etc., you'll find a place for your skills using online platforms.

- You can do your research while still in employment; find

out about the available opportunities and what you will need to start investing in passive income.

- You get to stay in-line with your values; when you have multiple streams of income, you won't be made to compromise your beliefs at any given time. You don't have that privilege when you work for someone else, and if you can't do what your employer is asking of you, then you end up losing your job. When you don't answer to anyone else, you can live by your values and freedom.

- You will have less stress and greater satisfaction. If you have children, having multiple streams of income means that you can work from home, spending as much time as possible with your children.

- You have room for taking risks; it will be harder to change careers or take serious business risks when you grow older since you will have family obligations. When you are an entrepreneur with multiple streams of income, you might make mistakes, but they will only give you an open mind-frame to know which decision to make in the future. Whatever the decision that you make, always do thorough research; you don't want to take risks blindly, do you?

- Your children's college fund: you can save the money that you earn from multiple sources of income to pay for your children's college fees in the future.

- Living a comfortable life; for you to create and sustain true wealth, you need to avoid extravagance. At the same time, it doesn't mean that you lack the basic needs for you to save. Creating multiple sources of income will give you an extra income that will enable you to save comfortably.

- Building long-term wealth: thinking about long-term benefits can be hard when you are earning very little in the beginning. The sacrifices that you make at the beginning with passive income streams will have tremendous capital gains and long-term effects. Many multiple streams of income are scalable and sustainable, making them great long-term income generators.

- Paying cash while making purchases; in many cases, people will take loans to purchase cars or houses. Having multiple streams of income makes it possible for you to save enough to pay for such items with cash instead of loans, which come with interest. It's a very simple concept: pay cash, pay no interest.

Facts about Creating Sustainable Streams of Income

- You don't need a lawyer or an accountant when you're first setting up a stream of income and having them translates into extra costs when you haven't yet started making money. One exception: you may need the services of a lawyer if you are getting in the real estate business; you will need drafts of some legal documents, i.e., leases.

- There is not specific number on the income streams that you can have; you can have as many as you can run comfortably. The only limitation could be time; how many hours in a day can you spare to get it going? New streams of income will require some management in the beginning.

- Don't overstretch yourself.

- No one wants to work actively forever; make use of the available opportunities to create avenues that will ensure that as you grow older, all you'll need to do is relax and watch as your accounts grow.

Some of the questions you need to ask yourself to gauge whether you will sustain multiple streams of income include:

- Do you have any understanding of technology and time leverage principles? Do you have the necessary skills to help you in the management of the multiple income streams?

- Do you have experience in managing or hiring staff to help you run the multiple income streams? If not, are you available to run the multiple streams of income by yourself?

- Do you have the street smarts, business expertise, and negotiating skills that are vital in competing on multiple investment and business fronts at the same time?

- Can you access any expert advice on the many financial and legal issues that you are likely to encounter when managing and putting in place multiple income streams?

The idea of creating and sustaining multiple streams of income isn't as complex as it sounds. You have all the necessary skills to see it through successfully, all you need is proper planning and dedication, and you get to earn your income, with time. It may not always be fun and easy, but when the first dollar shows up in your account, you will be all smiles!

Multiple income streams work best for people aiming at brighter financial futures. To be in a better position to sustain multiple streams of income, you must diversify your streams of income as much as possible. How about opening brokerage accounts and investing in mutual funds or ETFs? You may end up earning real returns that can help greatly in supplementing your income; this means taking risks since you may lose money, but then, you must try to be sure. Another option would be investing in peer-to-peer lending firms, such as the Lending Club. Picking investments that will work to your advantage is easy since you can learn from people who have already gone through the same, successfully.

As you continue creating a new stream of income, you'll realize that you have less time that you originally thought you had. You'll see that you need to create more streams of income —spending time on the outset, but in the end, freeing up more time while providing you with financial independence at the end of it all. Get out of your comfort zone and do something that you thought of as impossible. You may discover something new that greatly boosts your income.

Chapter 8: Things to Avoid When You Have Multiple Streams of Income

By now, we all know that the key benefit of multiple streams of income is primarily its consistency and security of one's income — mostly income from related and non-related sources. While financial security can allow you to do a lot of things; it can sometimes create an overindulgence in situations, which are not only unnecessary, but possibly damaging to your future.

Financial security means you have a bond portfolio that can create a lot of income that must be spent each year, giving you more opportunities for reinvesting and even expanding your portfolio. You will most likely not be affected by issues of inflation and recession, so you must venture into a more secure option. Of course, you can achieve this with thorough research, perhaps explaining why the same income stream can yield different profits in different locations. So many factors have been discovered that influence these, from social, environmental, and even physical factors. Having multiple streams already shows that you are an investor. You should, therefore, understand some dos and don'ts in your operation.

Some recommendations facilitate your growth while at the same time, some serve as a warning. The things that you should avoid serve as a precaution or protective mechanism to ensure that things are moving in the right direction. They can warn you about potential harm and situations that may lead to business collapse. Always be willing to learn and adjust to change within the changing market.

Consumers' tastes and preferences are also continually evolving; this can sometimes mean that the mode of operation is modified to suit consumer needs. It's because customer satisfaction is the key. When customers are happy with the product, and they love the product or service, they consume more and refer more. The things to be avoided, therefore, can help you prevent that negative market rating, build more relationships with your financial providers, and increase your income. This is the reason why we also need to learn and understand what to avoid when you have multiple streams of income. Your research serves to guide you in your operations and keep you from making obvious mistakes that could have been easily avoided.

Financial security and freedom can give you the freedom to do whatever you want because you can afford most things. However, consider the following list of mistakes often made by those with multiple streams of income.

Limit Diversification

Once you start experiencing the joy of having multiple streams of income, you may be tempted to reduce diversity and focus on whatever streams you already created. Limiting diversification is an enemy of progress. The income from multiple streams of income can help in diversifying passive income as well, thus more growth and benefits.

When something has gone wrong with one stream, the others will not likely be affected, thus, this will not likely have an effect on your freedom and lifestyle. You will still enjoy the things you love without great fear of potential financial risk.

A good example: If your streams are in the line of real estate, do not be scared to diversify in the range of online marketing, writing eBooks about real estate investment, or many others. Diversity creates growth, and once embraced, one can enjoy the full benefits. Diversification also allows one to leverage the available resources to build additional revenue. Always try to be flexible and spontaneous, doing your research; if you are convinced that the particular venture can work, then go for it.

Over-Relying on One Financial Institution

There are many financial institutions offering a multitude of attractive services to their customers. When you have multiple streams of income, consider also investing in diverse financial institutions; this is because the institutions are also in business, just like you. They are affected by the law of demand and supply, depending on their customers for survival. If you rely on one single financial institution, when it goes down, you will go down, too.

Another reason to avoid one financial institution is because of the various services they offer. Some offer loans for startups and expansion of business, others coffer insurance cover while others provide online money transfer.

Using different institutions means that you are going for the best in terms of service delivery of a particular thing; also consider the free financial advice; this is essential for your business.

Another advantage in using different financial institutions: no one place is tracking all your income streams. No one wants their financial institution provider to know their net worth. Financial institutions, especially those that offer lending services, have led to business collapse; this can happen when one realizes a loss, and they saved some money there as well as offer their assets as collateral. Using different financial means in case of eventual loss, you can still make a payment plan with another bank that the current one may not know of its existence.

Direct Marketing

I know this may sound crazy, but this is something that has helped so many people leverage their resources and in turn, created many more income streams. Direct marketing can indeed help you build on your marketing skills, database, and networks to generate additional income. Direct marketing help when you are just starting up, especially when offering another product line with little effort. As streams of income increase, direct marketing may not be viable, and you may find yourself using a lot of energy and wasting time, as well as not being able to reach all your target consumers.

When income streams increase, consider using other marketing tools like promotions, advertisement, change of packaging, and offering free samples for testing. If you have a real estate rental like Airbnb, consider creating a multiple-stay discount for returning customers. Be spontaneous and sometimes surprise a deserving family with a special treat and capture it for online media to draw attention to your good will. Peoples' interest grows when you incorporate an initiative that impacts people's lives.

Many companies have used this method where a portion of their profit goes to community service. Though it is not solely for marketing, people will recognize what you do and consider purchasing your products and services. Be creative and strive to reach a wide range of customer base over a short period. You can even use the income from one stream to do the whole marketing process for you. Direct marketing may not provide the desired feedback that you may need, and it can be tiresome and cumbersome. Use your consumers and other marketers for referrals and let them also earn a commission from additional sales. It will allow you to invest in even more extra income streams.

Investing in Several Income Streams at the same time

Perhaps everything is going well for you at the moment. Your online streams of income are increasing, you feel like you need to continue growing your streams to realize more profit. Creating additional simultaneous streams can create mayhem instead of the desired leverage, and this may have arisen from lack of resources to lay a solid foundation. Go slow and continue being systematic, waiting for the new venture to pick up and be sustainable before launching another one. If you invest in many streams at the same time, you will be like a baby learning running before they learn to walk. You may overlook so many things.

Being systematic means, you are keen on potential risks; you don't want to take many risks recklessly. Potential risks outweigh the benefits of your business, as these risks may transfer to other streams, affecting their income. Bear in mind that this is any investor's nightmare. It is not to suggest that multiple streams of income are wrong, but that they should occur systematically. You should plan for the additional streams of income the same way you designed the previous ones. Analyze the risks in the same way. In a nutshell, treat any additional stream the same way you did the first one to realize full success. By doing this, each new stream will be a learning experience and offer an opportunity for improvement and growth. Conducting research – just as you did with the first ones — means you take your venture seriously and give each the chance that they deserve. Choosing the systematic approach means you will have ample time to monitor your other streams and evaluate if things are going on in the right direction.

The big question is: How do you make cash from multiple streams of income without messing *everything* up? Creating several income streams is the only way you will achieve financial independence; however, it would be foolish to start running six, seven, or more streams of income right from the beginning. You'll need a solid foundation before you can think of diversifying.

Assuming that your business is stable and it's bringing in a decent amount of cash every month, you might want to cushion yourself from industry drops and changes by building other streams of income. Consider the following ways you can build new streams of income without ruining your core business.

Choosing the Right Moment

Running successful businesses requires effort and time. To establish another stream of income, you will need proper timing. The best time to create a new stream of income is during summer, as many people are not thinking a lot about their jobs, they are all about vacationing. During summer, it's quieter, making it an excellent time for exploring new business ideas. Never try to start new income streams when you are busy with other things; failing to dedicate time to the new income stream surely leads to failure.

Protecting Your Core Business

If you choose to expand too quickly, you are taking a major risk, and you will overstretch yourself. You must remember that the main business is the priority, i.e., the running business that is your top income-earner should be your first priority. You should always direct a greater percentage of your time to your core business; don't fall in the temptation of neglecting it completely as you create other income streams.

It's obvious that when you dive into new ventures, you're passionate, spending as much time as humanly possible. Don't forget where your income is streaming in from at this point. If you neglect your core business, it will collapse, and you will have *no source of income!* You can't be sure about when your new income streams will start bringing in any money.

Automating as Much as Possible

The biggest secret in success running successful multiple income streams is using automation as much as possible. Look for ways to make it easier to run your core business; it's the only way you will get time to run other streams of income. For example, if your main business is freelance writing, you can think of teaming up with another writer who can help you in marketing. It could be a small disadvantage in that you will incur the costs of paying your employee(s), but at the end of the day, you get time to explore new avenues of income. You can balance this out by making sure that you dedicate time and effort to the new income streams, which will enable it to make money in a shorter time. If it's necessary to hire people or someone to perform certain tasks for you, i.e., virtual assistant, don't shy away from the idea; you must spend money to create more income. Trying to do everything by yourself will end up consuming all your time, and in the end, it will be impossible to start or sustain multiple streams of income.

Working on Building Semi-Passive Incomes

If you already have a full-time job, it will be impossible to begin working on another full job due to time limitations. You only have 24 hours a day (and you must sleep sometime!) When you want to create a new income stream, you should think about setting up a semi-passive revenue stream.

For example, if your main business is online writing, and you write novels as your second income stream, dedicate more time to online writing, and spend two hours per day writing novels. Once you release your novel in the market, it will sell while you sleep and eat! This is a perfect example of a semi-passive income stream. It requires some work, but when it starts bringing in cash, you don't do anything to keep it running.

The right time to convert semi-passive income streams to passive income streams of income is when you have enough money to pay people to manage your business for you. It's better to begin with semi-passive income streams then convert them to passive income streams as you continue stabilizing.

Putting New Streams of Income on Hold if Necessary

People think that creating and sustaining multiple streams of income with the sole purpose of generating extra income is very easy; it's not as easy as that. You may not make a single penny when starting an income stream. If your core business requires more attention at any given time, don't shy away from putting other streams of income on hold until when you can create time for them. Don't compromise your main source of income for something you aren't sure is sustainable.

Common Mistakes Entrepreneurs Make When They Have Multiple Streams of Income

No Clear Purpose or Vision

Having no purpose or vision is the main reason that multiple streams of income fail. In many cases, people start new income streams without any clear purpose or goals; they don't have an idea why they are setting up the income streams or what they hope to achieve in the future. If you have no clear vision, you will give up when things get tough. Having vision and goals will give you something to work for, helping you hit your target.

Absence of Focus

If you try to do too much at one time, you are on the pathway to failure. Having focus makes it easy to communicate with your audience about the exact product that you are putting in the market. If you try to please everyone or add several features at once, you will end up mixing concepts and *diluting the message*. Take one step at a time.

You may be facing pressure from your team members, investors, or clients; you must teach yourself how to say no. Have a list of things that you want to do first, in the order of priority. In this way, you will be able to make better and wiser decisions concerning your additional streams of income and the core business.

Creating Products Nobody Wants

Many times, you may come across products that don't add any value to the user. These products may be trying to address a problem that isn't big enough or even one that doesn't exist; the solution that provide is not a solution at all. To avoid such scenarios, you must ensure that you are creating a useful and appropriate product for your target audience. Before you start creating a new income stream, take time for market exploration and research/development, finding out if there is the possibility of better opportunities that you can invest in to make more money.

Chasing Investors Instead of Customers

Having a perfect sounding investment idea for multiple streams of income doesn't necessarily mean that you'll get automatic funding.

The safest way to keep your new streams of income running is by drafting business models that allow your products to pay for themselves. Don't focus too much on building pitches; focus on building the streams of income. Look for customers who will pay for your products instead of focusing on funding. By doing this, the process of running multiple streams of income becomes easier and more stable.

Launching Too Early, or Too Late

Launching your new income streams too early or too late can be a fatal business idea. Ensure that your products have the basic levels of usability and design in their features. A balance between creating your products to perfection and early launching will give you huge benefits.

Shying Away from Asking for Help

Many entrepreneurs don't like asking for help, even when things are hard. Many people have been successful at running multiple streams of income; you can always seek their advice when you get stuck. You will find it easier steering in the right direction instead of wasting too much time in trial and error; the more you speak about the challenges you are going through, the easier it becomes to learn, using others' knowledge and mistakes to avoid your own.

Absence of Growth Plans

For your multiple streams of income to be successful, you must have a clear outline of your sales and marketing plans and the outcome that you hope to achieve in the long-term. The aim of creating multiple income streams is to create avenues for more wealth creation. You must lay down growth plans that will guide you on what you need to do and when, ensuring that you have tangible development plans that will facilitate long-term growth for your streams of income.

Chapter 9: Tips and Tricks of Creating Passive Income

Passive income means making money without participating in the process. Passive income doesn't mean that you get to use your cash while you are inactive; you can't collect money without working! The good thing about passive income is that it's a practical way to earn and provide you with freedom and security IF you are willing to put in the work.

Passive income refers to the income that you receive after having successfully set up a business that basically runs itself. You will have to commit your energy and time upfront to start enjoying passive income. Once set up and running, passive income is the money that you earn in a manner that doesn't require your daily input to keep it running. Some passive income ideas include starting and building a blog, renting out properties, etc.

Passive income comes with financial security; though you may have to risk when starting on passive income, eventually, it will prove to be a constant source of income, in the long run. You will always be sure that you have security since it won't consume much of your time.

Why Passive Income?

If you are an individual who is a forward thinker, you may be dreaming about leaving the formal employment sector to enjoy your retirement; you may even be thinking of early retirement. At the end of the day, if you dream without planning, you will be left with nothing but the dream.

A source of income that is hustle-free makes life a lot easier. Passive income is effortless and automatic once the money starts streaming in. As you are setting things up, it's time-consuming and tedious, however, with time, as the money starts flowing into your account, you begin relying less on active income. You will start believing that magic is real!

For many people, passive income means exiting the familiar rat race of waiting for payday at the end of every month; it means freedom. Something else you won't miss: long office working hours! You will be able to roam free, work, and live the way you want to.

It sounds like a perfect idea, by design. If you have a day job and you think that passive income is an impossibility, think again! It's possible, realistic, and achievable. You will only need to make little sacrifices in the beginning, before having the privilege of waiting for your paycheck to arrive while you do basically nothing.

Importance of Building Passive Income

Passive income is a great way of supplementing other sources of income. Formal income requires that you actively participate for you to get your pay. Even if you adore your job, the idea of earning an extra money without the commute, compromise of values, and always working for the other guy, well, it can be irresistible.

Benefits of Passive Income include;

- Speeds up your plan for building wealth
- Creates opportunities for early retirement
- Protects you from complete income losses if you lose your formal employment
- Provides an alternative source of income in instances where you can no longer work, or you exhaust your retirement fund

How Much Cash Can I Make from Passive Income?

You probably won't become a millionaire overnight. Many passive income ruses promise heaven on earth today; the only disappointment is that you might end up losing your life savings while trying them! However, if you can carefully execute passive income over time, you will end up making money — safely.

Habits of People Who Earn Passive Income Successfully

For you to start earning passive income, you will need to exercise patience and persistence. Consider the following traits you'll need to become a successful passive income earner.

Focus on Getting all the Extra Money Possible

The only way that you will have the motivation to work towards passive earning is by focusing on increasing your cash flow, then repeat, and repeat again. Begin by following different sources of passive income to see which one works best for you; this will push you to spot opportunities and control revenue. Making more money from passive income isn't as easy as it sounds, at least not in the beginning. Commit to researching your marketplace and product, being realistic about your options before using any startup capital for the venture.

Create Multiple Streams of Income

The only way that you will earn more from passive income is by increasing your sources of income; many people have three or more streams. You could choose to write a blog, engage in real estate, or sell digital products, to start. The more options that you can implement, the more money you are likely to earn from passive income.

Use Your Savings to Invest, Not Savings to Save

The reason why you should be saving money is to use the cash for investment; it's the only way that you will grow a business empire. It's good to exercise control when it comes to savings; you will need an amount for you to start in passive income. Put away money for emergencies but lock some savings in secure accounts so that you can't access these funds even in emergencies. By setting aside some amount of money automatically, you'll learn to survive without the money since you don't get to touch it. You can also save a portion of the money you earn from passive income, using it only to start another stream of passive income.

Be Decisive

Learn to make reversible decisions easily and quickly; this helps to conserve your mental acuity. Aggressively plan recurring actions to help in the execution of simple tasks automatically. You need to be decisive, so you aren't wasting time vacillating on which idea or ideas to pursue in terms of passive income.

Change Your Thinking about Money

To be a successful passive income earner, you need to change your beliefs about how you can earn money passively. Many people believe that becoming rich is beyond their control; successful investors know that earning extra income is an inside job, and you have the control.

Investing in Yourself

The wisest investment you can make is in your future; put your interest in learning about your investments before anything else. Look for mentors, listen to podcasts, and read all the available materials that you can find. Most successful passive income earners are avid readers. How will you invest in passive income if you have no idea of what passive income is all about?

Don't Rely on Steady Paychecks

Many of the successful passive income earners are not in formal employment; self-employment through passive income is the fastest and safest path to financial prosperity. You become more flexible when you are no longer in formal employment, having the freedom to make and implement financial decisions without having to consult anyone. What's more, you can invest in as many passive income ideas as possible, giving you the opportunity of making even more, instead of waiting for a certain amount of cash (your only paycheck) at the end of each month.

Set Achievable Goals

For you to make more money from passive income, you must have clear goals and specific plans on how you intend to achieve these goals. As much it is about passive income, you will have to do some work when you are starting. You must commit yourself to a target; this takes knowledge, effort, perseverance, and courage. Don't set unrealistic goals; they will only discourage you.

Associate Yourself with People Who Positively Impact Your Life

Stay close to people who share similar business sentiments, goals, and visions with you. When you attach yourself to people with similarly creative and smart minds, you will get more insight into better passive income avenues.

What are Some of the Passive Income Ideas in the Present Day?

Investing

You should think of your passive income and retirement plan as two separate entities. When people talk about passive income, many people think of investing since it produces huge benefits with very little input.

The main goal of investing for the long term is to generate income that you can use when you retire; you must ensure that you channel savings towards the retirement plan in your company. It's a good choice for consolidating a concrete retirement plan, but you will pay for penalties or taxes if you choose to withdraw your cash at any given time. When you enroll for a retirement plan, you need to wait until it matures to enjoy maximum benefits.

Real Estate

When you clear all your debts, and you have some savings left over, you can consolidate passive income by purchasing real estate assets and renting them out. Real estate is an excellent way of earning an extra income; it isn't among the most effective passive choices since you must put quite some amount of effort and time towards managing the property.

A good idea would be making your purchase close to where you live, making it more convenient to check on the property. Alternatively, you can look for a real estate agent who can advise you on the best place to purchase your property.

Before you buy your rental property, make sure that you first pay off for your home. Purchase your rental property with cash; don't ever borrow money to purchase a rental property.

Start a YouTube Channel/ Blog

If you have brilliant ideas that can appeal to a particular audience, you could create a YouTube series or educational blogs to produce online traffic. If you can come up with engaging content that attracts enough online traffic, you can sell d spots on the YouTube channel or ad space on the educational blogs. After completing the initiation process, you can now relax and start enjoying passive income streams.

Setting up profitable websites can be hard, mainly because there is stiff competition; it will require a lot of dedication for you to get a break into this online platform. The advantage of this venture is that it is inexpensive to set up, and the risks are minimal. The cost of setting your website up will only be paying for the hosting package; hosting companies such as Bluehost offer cheap packages from as low as $2.95 per month.

To earn passive income through your website, you must first research and learn about affiliate sales. You can link your products to Amazon affiliates; when a consumer clicks on the link and purchases the product, you earn money.

You can create passive incoming by passing on your knowledge to people through creating information products. You can use platforms like Skillshare or Udemy to begin selling online classes.

Build Information Products Funnels

Sales channels are powerful tools for earning passive income; they provide great potential for passive online income. If you can configure these funnels properly, you can start earning income at the comfort of your house very easily. However, you need to familiarize yourself with the conversion optimizations concept.

Coming up with appropriate hooks is the trickiest part when building information product funnels. There is stiff competition, since many people have already created funnels for many types of services and products

Do your research and find out what can be enticing to potential customers. Pick a unique product or service for a unique market. Observe the trends; find products that are popular, related to money or diet, etc. Find value addition to these products, and you can be sure that your passive income will start streaming in.

Sale of Digital Products

When you produce engaging content that will attract adequate traffic for you to host ads, you can create products that will catch the attention of your audience, as well. It could be an e-book or even an app that will keep generating passive income for you for many years to come.

Store Stuff for People

People are always looking for inexpensive options on how they can store their extra stuff. What could be a better passive income generating method than storing people's furniture, clothes – any item, really - for pay? You could consider purchasing storage facilities to venture into large-scale investment or using your shed or basement for a start. You only need to keep your clients' items secure and safe.

Rent out Items that You no Longer Use

You might have things that you no longer use, yet they are in reasonable condition. Others may need such items as a kayak, trampoline, a trailer; consider earning passive income by renting them out. Also, you can rent out extra space in your house by advertising on websites such as Airbnb and social media platforms. You only need to upload clear pictures and the set price of the items you want to rent out.

Launch Automated Webinars

Webinars are said to be among the most popular and efficient ways of earning passive income. Launching automated webinars can help you start earning passive income, however, before you launch one, become familiar with them by committing to one every week for about a year. Once your webinars begin to convert, then you can now automate them.

In some instances, you might be able to automate your webinars before a year; once they convert, they convert. The secret is targeting the right audience with the appropriate message. In many cases, automated webinars involve creating webinar funnels; these also include email sequences, up-sells, and self-liquidating offers.

As much as it sounds complicated, when they roll out, they are excellent money-making machines.

Earn by Getting Paid for the Time You Are Online

You can get passive income from certain sites by simply logging in to them, i.e., UpVoice will pay you for spending time on LinkedIn, Facebook, etc. All you need to do to start earning is sign up through Facebook; upon approval, you install the UpVoice browser on your

Chrome browser. It's a secure extension that doesn't affect the performance of your Chrome browser. You will be paid daily tokens by visiting the participating sites, namely:

- Twitter
- Facebook
- Amazon
- You Tube
- LinkedIn

You are even paid more if you participate in their surveys. You can buy gift cards using the tokens, i.e., VISA gift cards.

Designing Greeting Cards

Certain companies can pay you to design greeting cards for them; some pay as much as $300 for this service. There are online sites such as Card Gnome that you can use in the design process. All you need to do is to use these sites, design your greeting cards, and put them up for sale. Every time that someone purchases your greeting card, you earn 5% of the total amount. You get your cash once you earn $10.

Selling Your Photographs

Some of the photos you post on Instagram can get you more than just "likes." You can upload your photos to stock photography platforms. Your pictures don't have to be the professional type, but they do need to be realistic images. After uploading your photos, you will receive email notifications when someone buys your work. You may not make so much money instantly, but you can start by earning $5 on sites such as Foap. However, if you have a good camera, you can give photography some serious consideration.

Get Your Cash Back from Credit Cards

You can start earning income passively by signing up for credit cards that offer points or cash after you have paid the balance each month. Remember not to overspend; for this method to be passive, you must not be using money that isn't in your budget.

Selling Lesson Plans

The idea of selling lesson plans is particularly beneficial for teachers who are already writing lesson plans. You can put your lesson plans on platforms such as *Teachers Pay Teachers.* By doing this, you will be helping other teachers across the globe and at the same time, earning some income.

Sticking Ads on Your Car

If you are one person who drives a lot, you can place an ad on your car; this is a platform for earning passive income without any upfront costs. In a month, you can earn more than $100 from platforms such as Carvertise. Such companies favor Uber or other car hire service drivers, and such drivers have greater chances of being chosen if they drive in bigger cities.

Conclusion

Passive income isn't difficult to generate, and there are several avenues to generate money passively. If you have enough savings, investing in real estate is an excellent idea; you will start enjoying rental income in no time. You can also invest in dividend funds that will generate steady income for you.

However, if you don't have enough savings, making money from passive income will take time. You must invest your time in the beginning in order to get financial benefits in the future without working. You can still pursue passive income while still in formal employment, allowing you to care for yourself financially as you plan to expand your ideas for creating paths for passive income.

The list of ways in which you can create passive income is endless. As you explore the best possible method that will work for you, be keen on ideas having long-term positive results. Find out how other people are making money from the same methods. How much are they making? How long did it take them to see profits? How much start-up capital will you require? Don't rush into avenues that require a lot of start-up capital or those that promise you quick returns; doing this will bring your other financial goals to a standstill. Look for trustworthy, profitable, and steady ideas. When you know the correct avenues to approach, passive income is easy to generate; you follow simple steps, exercising patience, and in the end, you'll see progress. Most importantly, never borrow money to invest in passive income ideas.

Multiple streams of income are the surest ways of earning money from different sources at the same time. There are many ideas that you can explore: from online writing to selling digital products to e-book writing to personal car ads, and even more serious ides like real estate. Use the internet to research each idea that interests you, learning how you can start from scratch to create multiple income streams and what you can do to ensure that they keep running in the long-term.

There are very many reasons why you should consider investing in multiple streams of income; you get to enjoy financial security, yet you don't have to quit your day job. Many people have become millionaires by investing in about seven or more streams of income and running them concurrently. However, don't fall into the temptation of starting several income streams at the beginning; build one stream and give it time to grow and start earning money before creating another one.

Sustaining multiple streams of income will require dedication and focus; no one can build an income stream and expect millions overnight. You must remember that by building multiple streams of income, you are taking the risk of losing your capital; the streams may fail to bring in the income that you expect. Still, when all is said and done, investing in multiple streams of income is the only sure way to financial freedom!

www.ingramcontent.com/pod-product-compliance
Lightning Source LLC
Chambersburg PA
CBHW060431220526
45465CB00008B/3090